Power Tools for the 21st Century

By Dr. Richard Alan Miller

Power Tools

for the 21st Century

By Dr. Richard Alan Miller

01774

OAK Publishing

Organization for Advancement of Knowledge

OREGON, USA

Power Tools for the 21st Century

ISBN 978-0-9883379-2-3
Manufactured in the United States of America

Published by
OAK Publishing
1212 SW 5th Street, Grants Pass, OR 97526

Cover & Interior Design
Elleyne Kase

Chapter Plate Art
Cynthia Elmore

Editor
Christina M. Schumacher

In loving memory of Larry Norager

For general information on our other products and services please visit us at
www.richardalamiller.com.

OAK Publishing
Organization for Advancement of Knowledge

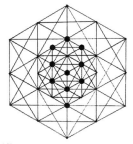

DEDICATION

To Mahalah Marshall-Rood,

as a good friend

an extraordinary visionary

a Renaissance-style artist

and her help in organizing our thoughts for this book

Contents

Workbook 1: EXERCISE SUPPLEMENT FOR
Power Tools for the 21st Century

Contents

Forward

BY DR. NICK BEGICH

Throughout my life I have met a number of interesting people around the world including innovator/researcher/author, Richard Alan Miller. He is a hyperactive personality with a wealth of knowledge he enthusiastically shares in lectures, radio interviews and through his writing. I met Richard at a Nexus Conference in the late 1990s and liked his childlike enthusiastic embrace of knowledge. I appreciated the way the material stimulated critical thinking in people on complex material that required careful listening and discernment.

Throughout his life Richard Miller has worked from both a classical science perspective and an occult, or hidden, side of knowledge. This book is truly about Power Tools and a few of them that come from this combined perspective. These are some of the things we can do to continue a shift in the paradigm of the future in a more productive direction first individually and then by simply discovering more of what we are as living souls. Richard and I share a world-view that suggests that we are much more than we think we are. Through my own life, and a very different path from his, I have come to similar knowledge about the potential of humankind. This book brings a combination of knowledge that can offer many new possibilities in inventing the next great version of oneself.

We are the driver's of our destiny by the way we "see" the world and recognize our full nature as created human beings. Choosing how we see reality and making the choices in our life's directions is awakening to our potentials. So this book opens the possibility of awakening our six senses through basic tested methods. It offers readers a way of being perhaps more greatly empowered by one's own possibilities in the context of your own values.

Our capacities as humans can be enhanced through recognition of our possibilities and then changing our beliefs about them. Faith comes from knowing, knowing comes from believing and believing creates our reality. Food, nutrients and electronics and high technology come together in this text that we launch readers on their own research in these various directions. As a basic blueprint for reforming the base upon which we see the world. This is a resource book that if readers will find useful in leading a more powerful and independent life.

Author & researcher Richard Alan Miller reveals a wealth and depth of knowledge and experience in three major fields; Alternative Agriculture, New Physics, and Metaphysics. Before many leading edge concepts became trendy topics, Miller has been in the international front lines of research, experimentation and documentation.

His focus on botanicals made him the leading world authority on herb farming, processing and marketing. With numerous books, bi-lines and websites, Miller's visionary work with Alternative Agriculture continues to be years ahead including concepts such as sustainability, intercropping, and forest farming.

Taking a step behind the scenes of "black ops" research is for most of us limited to speculations. Miller began working in that "X-Files" world in the 60s and has amazing experiences and conclusions to share. An original team-member, "man-in-black," Miller's research in the field of Parapsychology & Paraphysics began as a graduate physicist working 10 years with Army Intel/Pentagon.

During this period numerous foundational papers, including "A Holographic Concept of Reality" and *"Embryonic Holography"* were written. Richard Alan Miller's most recent work, *"Synthetic Telepathy and the Early Mind Wars"* discusses how some of his earlier work contributed to new "mind altering" technologies and their current applications.

His most recent works at Nexus Conferences in Brisbane, 2004, and Amsterdam, 2005 was titled *"The Non-Local Mind In A Holographic Universe."* He also has semi-technical papers to be presented in Anaheim at The World Nutra Conference in October, 2005. Title: *"Lab-Grown Cordyceps sinensis Hybrid: A Nano-Processed Medicinal Mushroom that Really Delivers."*

Offering fresh perspectives on Metaphysical traditions his books, papers & articles integrate his scientific research with time-honored metaphysical concepts, leading to such works as *The Modern Alchemist; A Guide to Personal Transformation and The Diamond Body, a Synergetic Approach to Mysticism.*

He brings a similar integration to *The Magical & Ritual Use of Herbs and The Magical & Ritual use of Aphrodisiacs.* Miller is listed in Who's Who in the World, America, and the West.

Enjoy the book and consider your own possibilities in what is the next evolution – The revelation of our own potentials.

— DR. NICK BEGICH, JUNE 2013

HISTORIC CONTEXT—*I had worked for DuPont and Boeing, and in biophysics at the University of Washington (Department of Anesthesiology - under Dr. John Bonica). It was there that I participated in the first studies in the U.S. on acupuncture. This was where my interests in herbology and Chinese systems of medicines began.*

I had been taught by eminent scientists such as Dr. Charles Muses (hyper-dimensional math) and Dr. Albert Szent-Gyorgyi (quantum biochemistry). Linus Pauling and Richard Feynman, on sabbatical from Cal Tech, were my first chemistry and physics teachers, (in the John Day Lecture Series at the UW).

Along with 12 graduate students, I even audited David Bohm's 1970 class in Quantum Geo-electrodynamics. *In graduate school, my thesis advisor was Dr. R. B. Murray, winner of the Nobel Prize in solid state physics. In that same period I also picked up such enrichment courses as Hellmut Wilhelm* Eight Lectures on Yoga and the I Ching.

The historic context is that the structure of this book is outlined and based on my education and background. This diverse set of backgrounds made me fertile ground for studies in the paranormal. I was essentially bred for this position with both my education and special interests.

By 1973, more than 25 scientists and six graduate students were working on various projects, primarily involving ESP and biofeedback studies. So, Seal Corp. wanted to develop a special group within the military, with skills verging on the paranormal.

These are the basic tools we discovered in the 1970s, to create supermen. They are now made available to duplicate that training (protocols), for use in our daily life. The goal, of course, would be take personal responsibility for our own evolution, by using the toys (power tools) of this century.

Introduction

"We should now proceed to find a neutral or Unitarian language in which every concept we use is applicable as well to the unconscious as to matter, in order to overcome this wrong notion that the unconscious psyche and matter are two things."

—PROFESSOR WOLFGANG PAULI

In physics, it is hard to reconcile the difference between the very large (like a galaxy) and the very small (like a microtubule). The laws we have discovered that govern the human-scale and the cosmos appear quite different from the laws which govern microbes and quantum mechanics. Yet the quantum world is the subtle essence of the cosmos, and does not differ in any way, or form, from it. So, at some level, the two become the same: "As above; So Below."

Likewise, at the human scale, often it is difficult to reconcile the great and small, the personal and the transpersonal, the particular or instinctual and the universal. The two meet in the human spirit. The characteristics of the cosmos are reflected in our inner lives.

If we choose to see the universe as holographic in nature, then physically, we share the exact same essence as the universe. There is a shift in paradigms where our perceptions move toward holistic visions; where our newer models in science eliminate previous basic conflicts between the sciences and religious beliefs.

Science used to claim we lived essentially as mechanical robots in a clockwork universe where religions maintained that man is ruled by more than matter alone. We are clearly not mechanical systems. In the spiritual view, mind-like or spirit-like factors make a difference in human behavior. New physics shows the dynamic entanglement of our conscious thoughts with the quantum representation of the physical world.

There is a hierarchy of observational levels or resolutions of self, others, and the world. Previously, they have included sub-quanta, quanta, photonic, atomic, electro-magnetic (EM), chemical, cellular, organism, consciousness, community, world, solar system, galaxy, and universe, now even a multiverse. Everything, including ourselves, is deeply connected in one holy movement reflected in the holographic concept of reality.

The dynamics of the very large and very small meet in the relationship of our bodies with the environment – local space-time. Spatial and temporal interconnections are revealed as fields within fields. The universal field exists everywhere and is often independent of time, taking the form of quanta or particles.

Shifting patterns of waves combine, dissolve, and re-combine. The psychophysical expressions of consciousness are revealed in their holistic complexity in our electromagnetic relationships at the planetary, temporal and universal level.

The nature of the very great and the very small meet in a mind-body connection where spirit becomes matter. Together, they form the immanent essence that has never been and can never be separated. On the grand scale, they meet when we confront both the spiritual and scientific nature of the Cosmos with its "unknown" mysteries.

These concepts and the philosophical approach are the basis of the worldview presented here. Taken together, they address some of the main issues in

OAK Publishing
1212 SW 5th Street
Grants Pass, OR 97526
(541) 476-5588

the scientific and spiritual domains. State of the art science is contrasted compared with ancient spiritual wisdom about living and being. Ancient om is contemporized and science becomes illuminative as in the days it alled natural philosophy.

fresh insights through these areas, we will emerge with an expanded ective of what it means to plumb both the mysteries of the universe and ysteries of the self. For, how can we know ourselves, if we don't have temporary grasp of the way the world works? Conversely, how can we ...ow the cosmos if we have failed to look within and understand, and directly experience, our own fundamental and spiritual nature?

Our place in the cosmos depends on the delicate interplay between the very big and the very small. Understanding that helps us comprehend how infinite pure potential becomes actualized as human consciousness and how, through a single tangible wave function, mind becomes matter. Waves of possibility are transduced into classical and macrocosmic forms.

Pardon us if we fail to come to any clear conclusions since the scientific models, cosmos, and ourselves are still works in process. It is for each of us to find a name for the power behind that process.

8-Circuit Model of Consciousness

Consciousness is a quality of the mind generally regarded to comprise qualities such as subjectivity, self-awareness, sentience, sapience, and the ability to perceive the relationship between ourselves and our environment. It is a subject of much research in philosophy of mind, psychology, neuroscience, and cognitive science.

Some philosophers divide consciousness into types of consciousness. The first is phenomenal consciousness which is experience itself. The second is access consciousness, which is the processing of the things in experience. Phenomenal consciousness is the state of being conscious, such as when we say, "I am conscious."

Access consciousness, however, is being conscious of something in relation to abstract concepts, such as when we say, "I am conscious of these words." Various forms of access consciousness include awareness, self-awareness, conscience, and stream of consciousness.

In common terminology, consciousness denotes being awake and responsive to our environment; these contrasts with being asleep or being in a coma. The term 'level of consciousness' denotes how consciousness seems to vary during anesthesia, and during various states of mind, such as day dreaming, lucid dreaming, imagining, etc.

Timothy Leary was an American writer, psychologist, modern pioneer and advocate of psychedelic drug research and use, and taught this at Harvard University during the 60's. As a counterculture icon, he is most famous as a proponent of the therapeutic and spiritual benefits of LSD. He coined and popularized the catch phrase, "Turn on, tune in, drop out."

The 8-Circuit Model of Consciousness is a replicable approach, or model of consciousness, proposed by Timothy Leary, the leader of the 1960's psychedelic movement. Leary believed the mind is best viewed as a collection of 8 "circuits", also called "gears" or "mini-brains". Each stage represents a higher stage of evolution than the one before it.

The first four, which Leary presumed to reside in the left lobe of the cerebrum, are concerned with the survival of organisms on earth. The other four, which Leary suggested are found in the right lobe, are for use in the future evolution of humans and remain dormant in the majority of human beings.

The Bio-Survival Circuit is concerned with the earliest modes of survival and the basic separation of objects into either harmful or safe. This circuit is said to have first appeared in the earliest evolution of the invertebrate brain. It is the first to be activated in an infant's mind. Leary says this circuit is stimulated by opioid drugs. This circuit introduces a one dimensional perception, forward and backward, i.e. towards food, nourishment, and that which is trusted as safe and backwards-away from danger and predators. [Survival = Khien Trigram]

The Emotional Circuit is concerned with raw emotion and the separation of behavior into submissive and dominant. This circuit appeared first in vertebrate animals. In humans, it is activated when the child learns to walk. Leary associates this circuit with alcohol. This circuit introduces a second dimension, up-down, linked with territorial politics and tribal power games. Up, as in swelling our body in size to represent dominance, and down, as in the cowering, tail-between-the-legs submissive stance. **[Emotional = Water Trigram]**

The Dexterity-Symbolism Circuit is concerned with logic and symbolic thought. This circuit is said to have first appeared when hominids started differentiating from the rest of the primates. Leary says this circuit is stimulated by caffeine, cocaine, and other stimulants. This circuit introduces the third dimension, left and right, related to the development of dexterous movement and handling 'artifacts'. **[Intellect = Air Trigram]**

The Social-Sexual Circuit is concerned with operating within social networks and the transmission of culture across time. This circuit is said to have first appeared with the development of tribes. Leary never associated a drug with it, but later writers have associated it with the drug ecstasy. This fourth circuit deals with moral-social/sexual tribal rules passed through generations and is the introduction to the fourth dimension - time. **[Social-Sexual = Earth]**

The Neuro-Somatic Circuit is the first of the right-brain "higher" circuits which are inactive in most humans. It allows us to see things in multi-dimensional space instead of the four dimensions of Euclidean space-time and is there to aid in the future exploration of outer space. It is said to have first appeared with the development of leisure-class civilizations around 2000 BC. It is associated with hedonism and eroticism. Leary says this circuit is stimulated by marijuana and Tantric yoga or, simply, by experiencing the sensation of free fall at the right time. **[Microtubule = Moon Trigram]**

The Neuro-Electric Circuit is concerned with the mind becoming aware of itself independent of the patterns imprinted by the previous five circuits. It is also called "meta-programming" or "consciousness of abstracting". Leary says this circuit will enable telepathic communication, and is impossible to explain to those who have only left-brain activity. It is also difficult to explain to those with active fifth circuits. It is said to have appeared in 500 BC in connection with the *Persian Silk Route*. Leary associates this circuit with peyote and psilocybin. **[Holographic = Fire Trigram]**

The Neuro-Genetic Circuit allows access to the genetic memory contained in DNA. It is connected to memories of past lives, the Akashic Records, and the collective unconscious, and allows for essential immortality in humans. This circuit first appeared among Hindu and Sufi sects in the early first millennium. This circuit is stimulated by LSD and Raja Yoga. **[Resonance = Khwan Trigram]**

The Neuro-Atomic Circuit allows access to the intergalactic consciousness that predates life in the universe (characterized as God or aliens) and lets humans operate outside of space-time and the constraints of relativity. This circuit is associated with Ketamine by Leary. **[Enlightenment = Sun Trigram]**

Leary's influence on my own works on consciousness is reflected in our current concepts today of memes, the way we break down events and situations into various categories for memory. While all things are basically the same (from an informational point of view), we tend to classify events and situations into such categories as "physical, "emotional," "intellectual, and so on.

As defined within memetic theory, a meme comprises a theoretical unit of cultural information, the building block of cultural evolution, or diffusion, that propagates from one mind to another. Biologist and evolutionary theorist, Richard Dawkins, coined the term meme in 1976. It is the way we organize our experiences from physical, emotional, intellectual, and so on.

Final Words (on how to use this book)

I have structured this book in such a way as to help organize various concepts and experiences. Often, it is difficult to determine which category some concepts might be considered. Like numerology or *Gematria* (Hebrew bible), the various chapters will represent various classifications of the information. This will help the organization and integration of the experience.

The I Ching, also called *"The Book of Changes,"* is the oldest of the Chinese classic texts. A symbol system designed to identify order in what seem like chance events, it describes an ancient system of cosmology and philosophy that is at the heart of Chinese cultural beliefs. It is also another form of meme classification similar to that used by Timothy Leary (and others).

I originally planned to have eight specific topics for each *Kwan* (or chapter), but this would have made this book far too large and cumbersome. So, I decided to take two of the more important topics for each meme and demonstrate how, when put in combination, they become a true Power Tool. While each was important, when used together, something far more synergistic is created, enhancing the quality of each meme.

The two topics selected for each chapter were also chosen to show the diversity of possibilities of what each Kwan might imply. This was done to help us pursue our Path with broader insight and direction. These will actually lead us toward taking more charge and responsibility for our life and the evolution of our own consciousness.

By making these changes in ourselves, so also will the world change. It is all about The Non-Local Mind and our "mind's eye." If we can see it there, it will become real. These are the tools which can help us toward our own True Will, and finding our own purpose in life.

1

SURVIVAL

KHIEN TRIGRAM

HISTORIC CONTEXT—*In the late 60s, psychedelic mushrooms were of interest to all those with any education and open minds. Back then mushrooms were being studied for their use in therapy and military (mind control) applications. This led me to write the book* Magical Mushroom Handbook *(1971), a basic field-guide for wild-crafting local and indigenous psychedelics.*

Thirty years later I chose to write about mushrooms again, as an entry into just how important metaphors can become for our use in the physical plane. Mushrooms have always been used as a food and medicine since time immemorial. Current-day studies now show mushrooms to be a direct cure and panacea for cancer, the heart, and diabetes – now the leading causes for death.

The historic context here will be how mushrooms have always been explored throughout history (Soma), as an enhancement *toward building a better physical body. We must have a sound physical body from which to launch other aspects of our Self. This aspect is the essence of survival, as represented by Adam Kadmon* (the Universal Man).

Chapter One

Cordyceps sinensis HEAA *(hybrid)* & Transfer Factor

Having worked in the herb trade more than 35 years, one gets to see various "new discoveries" come and go. Each year has always got something new (from bio-prospecting) ranging from St. John's Wort to Horny Goat Weed. Some of these may work but, mostly, they are just the soup d'joure (soup of the day for trendy markets). Once in a while, however, something hits the "radar," which is worthy of comment.

—DR. RICHARD ALAN MILLER; NUTRICON 2004, ANAHEIM, CA

It is often said that "We are what we eat," forming the foundation of our essence with diet and foods. So, any journey toward Higher Consciousness must begin with what we eat. That becomes the foundation from which all other aspects of self can emerge. Our groupings (like Survival) are basic metaphors, those primary drivers to make us become more than we are.

Cordyceps sinensis is a new generation of mushrooms now being used in the pharmaceutical industry and as a dietary supplement. *Cordyceps* is considered a "food" by the Food and Drug Administration (FDA), and classified as generally recognized as safe (GRAS). It is now considered a "Super Food" to be included in almost every diet. But, why are these rediscovered mushrooms considered super foods?

Since the dawn of shamanic healing, over 50,000 years ago, mankind has combed the globe looking for healing ingredients to concoct the ultimate panacea – a cure all. Long before the advent of modern pharmacology and wide-spectrum drugs, such as antibiotics, *Cordyceps* mushrooms were used along with many others.

The story of *Cordyceps* is a wild one involving a colorful pageant involving the Himalayas, dead insects, wild yaks, adventuresome natives, arduous journeys, Chinese Emperors, and diamondback rattlesnake venom! Any herbalist, or mycologist, has to agree that this is quite the profile for the life cycle of any botanical.

Exclusively reserved for royalty, such as Emperors, in ancient China, this treatment has an extraordinary and astounding history. Chemical analyses have shown that none of its alleged remarkable properties are superstition or mere folklore, but have now proven true. This is why this book opens with this food choice. *Cordyceps* represents the true essence of what constitutes a power tool for the physical plane.

Having worked in the herb trade more than 35 years, one gets to see various "new discoveries" come and go. Each year has always got something new (from bio-prospecting) ranging from St. John's Wort to Horny Goat Weed. Some of these may work but, mostly, they are just the soup d'joure ("soup of the day" for trendy markets). Once in a while, however, something hits the "radar," which is worthy of comment.

A new class of pharmaceutical mushrooms has recently attracted world attention through several new and very encouraging clinical studies. This newest host of mushrooms in the marketplace offer alternatives to the more conventional treatments for cancer and AIDS. We now know that cancer cannot exist in an oxygen-rich environment. This is true for all forms of cancer.

These medicinal mushrooms are extremely high in beta-glucans and polysaccharides in which both have been shown to be useful in cancer therapies.

Polysaccharides are long sugar chains with many oxygen sections within them. As these sugars are broken down by the body, the oxygen molecules are released and absorbed on a cellular level.

Without proper oxygen levels, the body is left to fall into degenerative states that encourage cancer, heart disease, immune disorders, and diabetes, and also allows many viruses to flourish such as Hepatitis C, Lyme's disease, and many others. This mushroom is extremely high in oxygen molecules.

The key is how to deliver oxygen to the body on a cellular level. This host of pharmaceutical mushrooms includes such well-known products as Reishi, Maitake, and Agaricus which are rich in beta-glucans which are known sources for oxygen. This list is continuing to grow with clinical studies now including more than 70 different mushroom species. The most interesting one to emerge is the *Cordyceps sinensis* which grows at about 16,000 feet in Tibet.

Cordyceps increases adenosine triphosphate (ATP) levels in the body by almost 28%. ATP is the body's energy supply source, the "body's battery so to speak", and is required for all enzyme processes. It is also now believed that ATP is where cold-fusion processes ("Brown's gas") occur in the body on a molecular level.

Although the concept of molecular level cold fusion is not the subject of this article, we believe this is the root of biological energy exchanges, which will be explored in future writings by the authors. Considering the impact on the energy state of this mushroom alone, would make this a true super food.

What makes *Cordyceps* important for use with cancer is that it contains beta glucans and polysaccharides. As the sugars break down, the numerous oxygen molecules are released on a cellular level with the result being that any cancerous materials present are immediately destroyed. Cordyceptin, one of the target compounds (nucleosides), inhibits the DNA repair mechanism and is probably responsible for its anti-viral (HIV) effect

Cordyceps sinensis, just beginning to fruit

Full Spectrum Chemistries

There is a lot of confusion today in the field of pharmaceutical mushrooms as to what form of mushroom product is the best for use. There are various components of the mushroom which have been used as separated compounds. Is it the fruit-body, the mycelium, or an extract standardized from some particular compound, which is responsible for the mushroom's properties? This question is not as straightforward as it seems.

Fruit-body - This is the mushroom that you see above the ground. It is the spore producing portion involved with reproduction. Basically, the fruit-body is equivalent to the flower of a plant. Fruit-bodies ONLY form in response to some stress from the environment.

Mycelium - This is the growth form of the organism under the ground where all of the life processes occur such as growth, feeding, competing for survival and some forms of reproduction.

Broth - In cultivated mushroom products, the mycelium can be grown either by fermentation (in a tank full of liquid "broth") or it can be grown on a solid substrate of some material that is found in the natural growth condition (cellulose).

For production of many mushroom derived drugs and health supplements, the compounds are extracted not from the mycelium, but from the broth that the mycelium is grown in.

As an example, there are a number of pharmaceutical drugs produced from **Shiitake:**

Lentinan (from the fruit body)

LEM (from the mycelium) and

KS-2 (from the residual culture broth - an extra-cellular compound).

To extract Lentinan from Shiitake mushrooms is a pretty straight forward chemical process. But, what about another compound present in Shiitake, the one called Eritadenine? This compound is useful in the treatment of high cholesterol while Lentinan is used for the treatment of cancer.

If you extract Shiitake by hot water, then use alcohol to precipitate out the polysaccharide fraction, the Lentinan is concentrated and the resultant product is effective for cancer treatment or immune stimulation. However, with this process, we lose the Eritadenine and the extract has no effect on blood cholesterol.

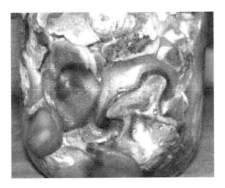

Shiitake, fruited and ready for harvest

So, even though a raw shiitake product shows great effectiveness in treating high cholesterol, the "Standardized Extract" available today is useless for this purpose. So what is the more valuable product - the raw Full Spectrum Shiitake or the "standardized extract"? The answer is neither, or both.

It really depends on what we are hoping to achieve with the supplement. For general health supplement usage, the best product is the one that has the greatest effectiveness over a broad range of conditions. In this example, it makes much more sense to use a full spectrum of products – the fruit-body, mycelium, and broth.

German precision created the concept of standardized extracts. But, now, we are beginning to realize that mixed chemistries play a more important role in the effectiveness of how unrelated chemistries might produce specific results. It is a complex form that is still not completely understood, but has clinical results not available in standardized extracts.

Adenosine and Cordycepic Acid

Most pharmaceutical mushrooms still use extracts for their most potent and most successful products and formulas. But, these are very specific and targeted extracts made for the specific purpose of concentrating specific compounds. Additionally, it is in these extracted chemical compounds that allow the rights to them to be held by the pharmaceutical patent medicine industry. Natural foods cannot be patented.

Chemistry

There are two general categories of bio-active compounds found in pharmaceutical mushrooms:

1. The polysaccharides which comprise most of the medicinal compounds. These are soluble in hot water and are not soluble in alcohol. The immune-stimulant type action so well known in mushrooms is from this class of compounds. If you are looking for Immuno-modulation action, then don't use alcohol extracts as they will not be effective.

2. Another class of compounds from mushrooms is those which are soluble in non-polar solvents like alcohol and hexane. These are usually smaller in molecular size and they are more specific in their bio-activity. Nucleosides, deoxynucleosides, and most of our antibiotics and anti-microbials fall into this category.

Medicinal Properties

Antibiotics: The medicinal properties of this mushroom are equally amazing. One of the highlights of modern research has been the discovery of novel new antibiotics in this mushroom. One of these, Cordyceptin, is very effective against all sorts of bacteria that have developed resistance to the other antibiotics.

Especially notable is its effectiveness against tuberculosis. It is also effective in all sorts of lung and respiratory infections as well as in the treatment of leprosy. All too many bacteria have, or are, developing resistance to the more common antibiotics such as penicillin (another fungus product).

Athletic Enhancer: The best known medicinal action of *Cordyceps* is for the increase of physical stamina. The Chinese national games in 1993 brought this mushroom to the attention of the world's sports authorities. A group of nine women athletes who had been taking *Cordyceps* shattered nine world records. The record for the 10 km run was beaten by an unprecedented 42 seconds. Not too bad in a world where records are usually broken by a few hundredths of a second!

There have been a number of stories of amazing improvements in sports performance. There has even been talk of banning *Cordyceps* from sporting events as an unfair advantage to those who can get it! Most professional athletes who use it now are unwilling to admit it due to the possibility that some sporting authority will outlaw its use.

In the other direction, the Canadian Olympic Committee has finally taken an official stand on Cordyceps. —They have ruled that it is allowed in professional competition.

Disease Therapy: Another major use of this mushroom is in the treatment of leukemia. It has shown outstanding activity against human leukemia in many trials in China, Japan, and elsewhere. One of the main uses in Traditional Chinese Medicine (TCM) has been for asthma and other bronchial conditions. Modern research now confirms these ancient traditional uses.

Clinical studies

Much of what is known about *Cordyceps sinensis* we owe to the research of Dr. Georges Halpern, a physician and professor emeritus with the University of Hong Kong and author of several books about Cordyceps.

Research suggests that *Cordyceps* may improve the bio-energy status of animals and, probably, humans. This happens because *Cordyceps* improves the internal balance mechanism, thus making the utilization of oxygen more efficient. These properties may account for the overall physical enhancement, the added endurance, and the anti-fatigue effects that are seen in humans using Cordyceps.

    1. Cordyceps Improves the Respiratory Function - Several scientific studies have demonstrated the benefits of *Cordyceps sinensis* in alleviating the symptoms of several respiratory illnesses including chronic bronchitis and asthma. In a double blind, placebo controlled study with 30 elderly volunteers *Cordyceps* significantly improved the maximum amount of oxygen these people were able to assimilate.

2. Cordyceps Increases Cellular Oxygen Absorption by up to 40% - Chinese studies showed that cardiovascular pharmacological studies of ethanol extracts of *Cordyceps* mycelia, and *Cordyceps* fermentation solutions, caused a change in the biological terrain that allowed for this increase in oxygen absorption.

In addition, studies also showed the effect of these compounds in relieving chronic obstructive pulmonary disease conditions by lowering cholesterol levels.

3. Cordyceps Improves the Functioning of the Heart - Numerous studies have demonstrated the benefits of *Cordyceps sinensis* on heart rhythm disturbances such as cardiac arrhythmias and chronic heart.

An even more vigorous study was conducted using "in vivo" mouse model induced acute Pulmonary Edema (Pneumonia) which causes systemic lack of oxygen, acidic body, and death. Research results show that animals taking *Cordyceps* had a significantly greater survival rate of 20% mortality vs. 80% mortality. This is a startling 400% improvement.

4. Cordyceps helps Maintain Cholesterol - A number of excellent studies have demonstrated that *Cordyceps sinensis* helps to lower total cholesterol by 10 to 21% and triglycerides (neutral fats) by 9 to 26%. At the same time it helps to increase HDL-cholesterol ("good cholesterol") by 27 to 30.

Blood Cells – Improves Blood Cell Viability & Function.

Genetic – Promotes DNA Repair

Liver Protection – *Cordyceps* improves liver functions, and helps with hepatitis and cirrhosis sub chronic and chronic hepatitis. These related liver diseases are more prevalent than most realize. Liver is the living filter of the human body, cleaning the blood and all other fluids of impurities. There is no way for you to survive, much less feel healthy, without a functioning liver.

Clinical trials on 33 patients with Hepatitis "B" and on another 8 patients with cirrhosis of the liver taking *Cordyceps* supplement, showed a 71.9% improvement on "Thymol Turbidity Test" and 78.6% improvement in" SGPT Test." Both of these are enzyme tests showing improving functions of the liver.

    5. Chronic Kidney Disease Improvement - Chronic kidney disease improvement of 51% were achieved after only one month with *Cordyceps* as a dietary supplement.

    6. Cordyceps Reduces Tumor Size in Cancer Patients - Several clinical studies have been conducted in China and Japan with cancer patients. The studies were done with *Cordyceps* using a therapeutic dose of 6 grams per day.

In one study with 50 lung cancer patients, *Cordyceps* was administered in conjunction with chemotherapy, tumors reduced in size in 46% of patients. A study in cancer patients with various types of tumors found CSE (6 g/day for over 2 months) improved subjective symptoms in the majority of patients. White blood cell counts were maintained and tumor size was significantly reduced in about half of the patients.

Researchers in Japan reported that *Cordyceps* enhances the general reactivity of the immune system in individuals with cancer. To discover this, they subcutaneously injected mice with cancerous (lymphoma) cells and then orally administered Cordyceps. This lead to a reduction of tumor size and prolonged the life of the person. *Cordyceps* also improved the antibody responses in these studies.

    7. Immune System - *Cordyceps* increases Natural Killer (NK) cell activity, increasing T cell production, which results in increased muscle mass. It also increases the power of muscles by building healthy younger cells.

Cordyceps effectively recharges the protective army of NK cells. The body's ability to fight infections and tumors depends on the availability of Natural

Killer cells. These are essential as the first lines of defense for maintenance of the body's protection mechanisms commonly known as the Immune System.

Several scientific studies of *Cordyceps* have especially focused on Natural Killer (NK) cells and *Cordyceps* effect on them as they relate to cancer formation. One in-vitro study demonstrated *Cordyceps* adding significant enhancement of NK cell activity in normal individuals as well as leukemia stricken people.

Chinese Journal of Integrated Traditional Western Medicine showed that natural *Cordyceps* enhanced the NK cell activity of normal patients by 74% and increased the NK activity of leukemia patients by 400%. Similar improvements of NK cell activities were found in large melanoma tumors.

The improvements in the Immune System were so impressive that Dr. Zhu at the Journal of Alternative and Complementary Medicine, 1998, stated: "Because of the above profound influence on immune functions, natural *Cordyceps* products have been used in many clinical conditions in patients with altered immune functions."

8. Anti-Aging – *Cordyceps* is an anti-aging fighter with numerous clinical studies. In controlled studies, elderly patients suffering from fatigue and some senility related symptoms reported relief in these areas. It was reported, after using *Cordyceps* for thirty days, to he reduce fatigue 92%, feeling cold 89%, and dizziness 83%. Patients with respiratory/breathing problems felt physically stronger and some individuals were able to jog up to 600 ft.

9. Cordyceps Protects against Free Radical Damage - Several studies have shown that *Cordyceps sinensis* protects against the damages caused by free radicals and has powerful antioxidants.

10. Cordyceps Reduces Fatigue - Several studies with animals have demonstrated that *Cordyceps sinensis* increases the cellular energy production and oxygen supply. A double blind, placebo controlled investigation showed a marked reduction in fatigue in elderly patients when they were given three grams of *Cordyceps* daily.

25

In another study, *Cordyceps sinensis* improved shortness of breath and reduced fatigue in patients suffering from chronic heart.

11. Cordyceps Helps Discomforts from Tired Legs - Several studies have shown that *Cordyceps sinensis* improves the flow of blood in the body by relaxing the smooth muscles of the blood vessels allowing them to expand. *Cordyceps* also improves the functioning of the heart and lungs.

Cordyceps therefore prevents or reduces the contraction of blood vessels which interferes with the flow of blood vessels in the legs, the main cause of tired.

12. Endurance & Stamina – The use of *Cordyceps* also reduces muscle soreness, enhances recovery, and promotes better oxygen efficiency in the body. One study fed rats *Cordyceps* while another group was fed a placebo. Both were placed in water and left to swim until failure. Those fed *Cordyceps* were able to swim 4 times longer than the other before failure.

13. Cordyceps Improves Stamina and Athletic Performance - Increases ATP synthesis, promotes faster energy recovery, reduces fatigue, improves physical function, and provides more stamina in people. Several studies with animals have shown that *Cordyceps sinensis* increases the cellular energy production and oxygen.

A study with mice demonstrated their improved swimming capabilities after six weeks of *Cordyceps* supplementation compared with a control group.

14. Cordyceps radically Increases Cellular Energy - Cellular energy, which is also known scientifically as the ATP/IP ratio, is positively affected. *Cordyceps* has been clinically proven to increase cellular Bio-Energy by as much as 55%.

15. Cordyceps Combats Sexual Dysfunction - Three separate Chinese double blind and placebo-controlled studies with over 200 men with "reduced libido and other sexual problems" showed remarkably similar results. On average, 64% of the Cordyceps-users reported significant improvement at the conclusion of the experimental period compared with 24% of the placebo group.

In another double blind placebo-controlled study conducted with 21 elderly women with similar complaints, 90% reported improvements of their condition following the use of Cordyceps. The control group showed no improvement.

16. Hormones (Adrenal, Thymus, and Mitochondrial Energy) - Dramatic natural improvements are seen in endocrine hormone levels, in fertility, and in sexual libido for men and women.

17. Sexual Function - Improves libido and quality of life in both men and women, fights infertility, increases sperm count, and increases sperm survival.

(1) Research on animal studies shows *Cordyceps* increases natural sex hormones.

(2) Prevention and improvement of adrenal glands, thymus hormones, and the infertile sperm count improved by 300% after *Cordyceps* supplement was used.

(3) Human clinical studies involving 189 male and female patients with decreased libido and desire showed improvement of symptoms in 66% of the cases.

(4) Another double blind study by the Institute of Materia Medica in Beijing, China showed female improvement of libido and desire of 86%.

(5) The most dramatic physical proof came from a fertility study involving 22 males that showed that *Cordyceps*, as a supplement, increased 33% sperm count, decreased by 29% the incidence of sperm malformations, and resulted in a 79% increase in the survival rate after eight weeks of use.

18. The Study In Ghana for Use with HIV - A study in Ghana, in 2004, involving 3000 early stage HIV patients were given a formula with *Cordyceps sinensis* (as a primary ingredient). At the end of six months, beyond anyone's wildest dreams, all 3,000 patients showed "no presence in their blood of HIV."

It has been long understood that the beta-glucan class of compounds found in many species of mushrooms significantly enhances human immune function. These classes of compounds are, in fact, the most widely prescribed anticancer medications in the world. The pharmaceutical drugs Lentinan, PSK and Grifolan are examples of this class of compounds.

Nano-Particle Milling

Nano-technology is the science and technology of materials at the nanometer scale (one billionth of a meter). This world of nano-scale objects is explored with high speed computers and powerful atomic resolution microscopes. In this realm, the rules of quantum physics provide matter with remarkable properties. Understanding and harnessing these properties will lead to technical breakthroughs in many fields of science in the 21st Century and will be as revolutionary as electricity, antibiotics, plastic and computers were in the 19th and 20th centuries.

The term nano-particle is generally used to indicate particles with dimensions less than 100 nanometers. For comparison, a human hair is about 50,000 nm in diameter, while a smoke particle is about 1,000 nm in diameter. The smallest nano-particles are only a few nanometers in diameter. These particles, called quantum dots, can possess properties that are entirely different from their parent materials.

Powdered medicinal mushrooms have been in the market for a long time, but newer nano-mesh myco products allow for optimal absorption in the body of the effective compounds. With less waste, dosage volume can again be lowered. Normal digestion will only allow upward of 38% absorption of material, but a product that is almost 1,000 times smaller than the cell wall will offer upward of 98% absorption.

This represents a particle size so small it can virtually penetrate the skin without chemical aids or solvents. Nano-particles amazingly absorb right through the spaces between the cells with three times the absorbability, economically reducing dosages to up to one third of a normal dose – less becomes more.

As size is reduced, a number of things occur. Absorption in the body is improved. Also, the surface area covered increases dramatically. Visualize a one inch cube and add up the six sides and we get six square inches of surface area. Slice the same one-inch cube into a billion thin slices and we now can cover two billion surface inches (front and back of each slice). This is why less is more. We still have the same one-inch cube but, now, instead of six square inches of coverage we can cover 308 football fields.

Nano-technology provides improved activity levels and allows ingredients to be suspended in clear beverages that, otherwise, could not be used because they could not be held in suspension. The nano-particles of *Cordyceps* further enhances the stability of the products, generally for a pH of 2, thereby achieving thermodynamic stability which allows pasteurization, control of reaction rates, and reduces browning.

Cordyceptin and DNA

There is evidence of another mechanism at play in the *Cordyceps* anti-tumor response besides the well-known immune modulation triggered by the polysaccharide compounds. It is related to the structure of at least some of the altered nucleosides found in Cordyceps, exemplified by the compound Cordyceptin [3'deoxyadenosine]. This is a molecule almost identical to normal adenosine with the exception that it is lacking an oxygen atom on the ribose portion of the molecule at the 3' position.

The same lack of this 3' oxygen can be seen in other *Cordyceps* compounds as well, such as Dideoxyadenosine. The lack of oxygen, at this particular position, is thought to be important in a very specific way. The structure of DNA depends on this oxygen to create the bond between adjacent nucleosides. This bond is between the 3' and the 5' positions on the ribose portions of the nucleosides, effectively forming the 'ladder structure.'

In the replication of any cell, the first step is the separation (like unzipping) of the DNA molecule down the middle between the pairs of complimentary nucleosides. The next step is the insertion, one at a time, of new complimentary nucleosides. These form hydrogen bonds between the complementary pairs and form phosphate-sugar bonds. This, in essence, is the structure that holds the DNA together.

The synthesis of the new DNA molecules proceeds with the sequential insertion of new compliment nucleosides one at a time into the newly forming DNA molecule. This happens until the original strand of DNA is replicated twice. Each of these replicated strands are exact copies of the original and forming the genetic code for a new generation of cells.

This synthesis continues to proceed with the insertion of each new nucleoside unless a 3'deoxyadenosine (Cordyceptin) molecule is pulled in.

When this happens, there is no oxygen present at that vital position to form the 3'-5' bond and the replication of the new DNA molecule stops. Once the DNA synthesis stops, the cell cannot continue to divide and no new cell is formed. In normal mammalian cells, this insertion of the deoxygenated adenosine is of little importance as healthy cells have an inherent DNA repair mechanism.

When this sort of error occurs, the altered nucleoside (the Cordyceptin) is removed from the string of nucleosides and a new segment of adenosine is inserted. However, by their very nature, cancer cells have lost this DNA repair mechanism. If they could correct their DNA errors, they would not be cancer cells.

Most bacteria, including the HIV virus, lack this DNA repair mechanism. When we look at the rate at which cancer cells replicate, it is clear how this mechanism could exert a significant anti-tumor response. For example, normal healthy breast tissue cells have an average life span of about 10 days, after which they reproduce and a new cell is formed.

But, breast cancer cells multiply much quicker than healthy cells. They reproduce themselves on average every 20 minutes. This means that the breast cancer cells are replicating about 750 times faster than the surrounding healthy tissue. If the Cordyceptin were equally toxic to both types of cells, it would be killing off the cancer cells 750 times faster than the healthy cells.

Due to the DNA repair mechanism in the healthy cells, Cordyceptin appears not to interfere with the healthy cell replication and the tumor-cell kill rate is actually much higher than the 750-to-1 ratio.

The same sort of DNA interruption mechanism is responsible for the anti-tumor effects of some other chemotherapy agents as well. This same mechanism of DNA synthesis inhibition is probably the responsible mechanism for the anti-viral effects seen with Cordyceptin.

Conclusions

The best known medicinal action of *Cordyceps* is for the increase of physical stamina. Cordyceptin is very effective against all sorts of bacteria that have developed resistance to other antibiotics. *Cordyceps* improves the internal balance mechanism, thus making the utilization of oxygen more efficient.

Numerous studies have demonstrated the benefits of *Cordyceps sinensis* on heart rhythm disturbances such as cardiac arrhythmias and chronic heart failure.

Four excellent studies have demonstrated that *Cordyceps sinensis* helps to lower total cholesterol by 10 to 21% and triglycerides by 9 to 26%. At the same time, it helps to increase HDL-cholesterol ("good cholesterol") by 27 to 30%.

Human clinical studies involving 189 men and women patients with decreased libido and desire showed improvement of symptoms and desire of 66%. The most dramatic physical proof came from a fertility study involving 22 males that showed that *Cordyceps* as a supplement increased sperm count by 33%, decreased by 29% the incidence of sperm malformations, and resulted in a 79% increase in survival rate after eight weeks of use.

In humans using Cordyceps, these properties and others may account for the overall physical enhancement, the added endurance, libido enhancing and the anti-fatigue effects.

Worldwide studies have shown that this unassuming fungus delivers even more potentially life-enhancing benefits than claimed. This is a super food which is just beginning to make it into western literature. The reduction of this material in size as a nano-particle also has great promise as a new delivery system for the pharmaceutical trade.

Further research work continues to be conducted which may lead to additional patent medicines. More importantly, the full-spectrum of compounds present in the fruit-body, mycelium, and broth of the natural substance, continues to prove, once again, that ancient knowledge meets the modern test of science.

Transfer Factor

An Alternative Approach to Antibiotics

In 1949, Dr. H. Sherwood Lawrence was working on the problem of tuberculosis. What he was trying to discover was if any component of the blood could convey a tubercular sensitivity from an exposed recovered donor to a naive recipient. Whole blood transfusions could be used, but only between people of the same blood type.

Lawrence first separated the blood's immune cells, the lymphocytes or white blood cells, from the whole blood. Then, he broke open the lymphocytes and separated the contents of the cells into various size fractions. What he found was that a fraction of small molecules was able to transfer tuberculin sensitivity to a naive recipient. This is what Dr. Lawrence called *transfer factor*.

Transfer factors are tiny protein molecules that are produced by immune cells called T-cells. It allows the immune system to remember conditions for which immunity has already been established. For example, when a person has been infected with chicken pox in childhood, their body develops a memory of that illness, and prevents the person from becoming re-infected with it later in life.

In the future, the specific immune *transfer factor* molecule for chicken pox will endow the immune system with the exact 'blueprint' of what chicken pox looks like, and the body will be able to quickly recognize and respond to any possible re-infection. Many of these *transfer factor*, or "immune memory molecules," were introduced to us from our mother's milk, or colostrum, which is the richest source of concentrated *transfer factor*s known to scientists.

*Transfer factor*s in colostrum have the sole purpose of transferring immunity from the mother to the baby's immature immune system. All mammals produce *transfer factor*, but scientists prefer to work with chicken and normal bovine colostrum. A healthy cow already produces millions of different *transfer factor*s, but when the cow comes into contact with a pathogen such as a virus, it produces a new *transfer factor* for that specific virus or pathogen.

For individuals challenged by specific pathogens, such as those suffering with chronic illnesses like *"Chronic Fatigue Syndrome,"* supplementation with the appropriate *transfer factor* molecule may provide the 'missing link. This would allow the immune system to target and destroy the offending pathogen, and mitigate the symptoms of the disease

Soon after giving birth, female mammals produce colostrum which is a milk-like substance that jump-starts a newborn's immune system. Researchers now believe that the benefits of colostrum do not necessarily end there. If we have a compromised immune system or are just looking for a boost to our healthy immune system, colostrum may be the jump-start we need to fight infection or immune-related chronic diseases such as cancer.

Transfer factor is a set of messaging molecules that convey immune information within an individual's immune system. Nature also uses *transfer factor* to carry immune information from one individual's immune system to another individual. This, in fact, is how it got its name: by being the factor that transferred immunity from one person to another.

Transfer factor may become a valuable way to treat communicable disease in the future as researchers learn more and gain the ability to isolate specific factors. In fact, *transfer factor* may someday cure the diseases ravaging the world population such as AIDS and Ebola.

After the tragic 2002 Ebola outbreak in Uganda, freelance journalist Sam Wainaina explored the potential benefits of *transfer factor*s in Africa. In his article, Wainaina concluded that had *transfer factor*s been used during the outbreak, it could have been contained sooner, saving lives and avoiding mass hysteria.

Originally blood was the only source of *transfer factor*. It was not until the mid 1980's that two researchers came up with the idea that *transfer factor* may also be present in colostrum. The confirmation of this discovery was awarded a patent in 1989. Colostrum is now the best source of *transfer factor*.

Those who have worked with cattle know that if a calf is not allowed to nurse from its mother it will most likely die within a short time. The calves would die in spite of an abundance of food. Death, in these cases, was cause by infections brought on by the most common organisms. For whatever reason, the immune systems of these calves were not working. Seeing this suggests that there is some kind of immune information being transferred from the mother and her infant.

Milk allergies are caused by the large milk proteins, primarily casein, and to a lesser extent, the immunoglobulins. These proteins are completely removed from the *transfer factor*. Lactose intolerance is most common in Oriental populations; much less so in those of European or African decent. *transfer factor*s themselves are non-allergenic. Common allergens such as immunoglobulins and casein are removed from *transfer factor* products.

Transfer factor is good for everyone who needs an extra immune boost. The three groups who are most in need of immune strengthening are the young, the old, and anyone under stress. Almost all of us fall into one of these categories. We often talk of the baby-boom generation. Most of these people are at an age where already their immune systems are becoming lax. *transfer factor* is a way to boost a lagging immune system.

Matrix Immune Booster (MIB)

Most sources of *transfer factor* are from colostrum and egg yolk for the derived antibodies. Matrix Immune Booster (MIB) is a patented concentration of *transfer factor*s and other natural components from cow colostrum and egg yolk. Those immune modulators include:

IP-6 (Inositol hexaphosphate) aka Vitamin B-8
Soya bean extract (Phytosterols)
Olive leaf extract (Olea europonea)
Mannans (from Aloe Vera leaf)
Cordyceps sinensis HEAA (hybrid) – (*hetero-polysaccharides*)
   + other pharmaceutical mushrooms and nutritional support

Transfer factor, also known as the "immune memory molecule," is a small peptide with three main functions involving mainly the T-lymphocytes. These are small white blood cells crucial to the cell mediated immune response. These functions are:

Transfer - Once the *transfer factor* contacts the lymphocytes of the animal or human, it sits on top of the H-Like receptor and, along with this receptor, now becomes "the unique antigen-specific recognition" area. It transfers the antigen recognition from "educated" to naïve lymphocytes (from Mother to offspring in colostrum).

Induction - Only occurs in the presence of a pathogen. This increases white blood cell activity, cytokine, and chemical messenger production. It turns on antigen processing cells (APCs) and microphages.

Modulation - Reduces oxidative and immune-mediated damage to the host. This is done by inducing T regulator cell activity. It sends message that the pathogens have been successfully eliminated. It also plays a role in control of allergy symptoms and autoimmune disease. It also tends to favor cell mediation over antibody production. This prevents the immune system from harming the host.

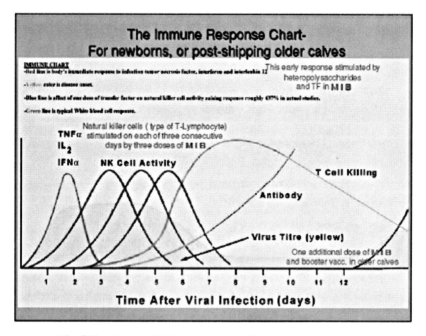

The following results involved more than 50,000 head of cattle from 2002 farm studies to the present

One thousand grams of fresh cow liquid colostrum contains about 170 grams and less than 0.8 gms total *transfer factor*. The sizes of these ingested antibodies are very large complex structure proteins about 150,000 molecular weight. Also, less than 15% are absorbed in the GI tract after gut closure. The MIB is a very small linear protein, about 4,400 in molecular weight, and more than 85% is absorbed in the GI tract at any age.

What makes the real difference is the addition of hetero-polysaccharides. These are sugar molecules hooked together in long, branching chains. They come from a hybridized form of *Cordyceps sinensis*, grown in laboratory conclaves. In part, they work by stimulating the toll-like receptors on antigen processing cells and dendritic cells and by stimulating cytokine production.

Natural Killer Cell Inductor

Transfer factor is also a natural killer cell inductor. These cells are non-specific attack cells that seek out and destroy infected or malignant cells and cells infected by viruses.

Transfer factor increases natural killer cell activity five times over normal rates and it is non-species specific. It is believed that this aspect of *transfer factor* is related to the significant improvements seen in certain cancer patients that have taken this product. Multiple sclerosis patients have also shown improvements.

Transfer factor in cats, dogs, horses, cows and humans is virtually identical structurally and completely identical functionally. This has helped in the production of this product since cows can produce large quantities of colostrum that is then used for extraction of *transfer factor.*

Suppresses immune function

Transfer factor is also a suppressor of immune function. It is paradoxical that the same product can both stimulate and suppress immune function, but, transfer function depends on the specific antigens and the status of the immune response. *transfer factor* can stimulate the release of T suppressor cells when "down" regulation is necessary due to over activity.

Autoimmune diseases, chronic obstructive pulmonary disease (COPD) and allergic reactions are situations where our own immune response has over-responded to antigenic stimulation. *transfer factor* works in these situations because it can slow down this overactive response.

Obvious advantages

While discussions of the immune system tend to be fairly technical, the practical advantages of a potent new immune stimulating treatment are obvious.

The ability to stimulate our body to attack and destroy bacteria and viruses will reduce the amount and types of antibiotics that may need to be used. It is important to try to retain those antibiotics that are available to veterinarians and to use them in a way that will maintain their effectiveness for as long as possible.

If veterinarians can stimulate a better immune response to respiratory bacteria, skin pathogens and various viruses, then the need to use antibiotics is lessened. If *transfer factor* can produce such boosts in immunity in 24 hours, then the potential for use as a pre-travel protectant, or a post-exposure treatment, is tremendous.

Horses suffering from other diseases such as Cushing's disease, laminitis, colitis, cancers ranging from sarcoidosis to melanomas, and reproductive conditions such as chronic metritis, may all benefit from *transfer factor* use. This product may indeed be the long-awaited next step and the field of immunotherapy may finally fulfill its promise.

While studies have not yet been concluded for FDA approval for use in human dietary supplements, it is quite obvious how *transfer factor* will find use in the treatment of cancer and overall total health programs.

2

EMOTIONAL

WATER TRIGRAM

HISTORIC CONTEXT— *In 1972, Elmer Green (Menninger Foundation) wanted to test Jack Swartz (Portland, OR). He could put large needles through his arm and then stop the bleeding at will. This immediately became a primary military area of interest and opportunity, understanding how to stop bleeding with the mind.*

This was one of the very first times biofeedback equipment was used for enhance performance *with military personnel, and where the concept of a* super soldier *first originated. The* Seal Reports *is a new book on the 12 reports generated for Seal Corp., the precursor of what later would be later known as Navy SEALs.*

The historic context here is how training the brain (using video and audio feedback loop) was about how the Higher Self *communicates with the conscious mind. Emotions demonstrate a higher detail of the physical world, and can be used to* enhance performance.

To be able to control heart rate, pulse, and respiration allows another level of dialog with consciousness. Since cetacean seem to have a higher form of awareness, they represent where we can go when connected more to the emotional aspects of our awareness (metaphor).

Chapter Two

Biofeedback &
Brainwave Training

"Gentlemen, I have a confession to make - half of what we have taught you are in error; and furthermore we cannot tell you which half it is."
— SIR WILLIAM OSLER [*to a graduating medical class*]

Richard Caton (1842–1926) first discovered electrical rhythms within the brains of animals in 1875. It was over 50 years later when Hans Berger showed that man also had these rhythms. His original search began with the hopes of finding the physical link between man's mind and his body.

It was this mind/body question which led Berger to dedicate his life to finding this link. He became interested in the work of Caton, and others, and set up his own laboratory to further investigate the electrical activity of the brain. After 20 years of research, he was able to record the brain rhythms of a human.

He spent another 10 years convincing his colleagues that this rhythm came from neurons of the brain, not from blood flow or connective tissue. His original studies also showed that this rhythm changed with age, was vulnerable to sensory stimulation, and was affected by chemistry.

World War II broke out and Hans Berger never finished his original work which involved cracking the code of brain rhythms and their link to "psychic functions." Since that time, no one else has either. Research was centered on the more practical applications of the electroencephalogram (EEG), especially to epilepsy, brain metabolism, brain functions, and levels of consciousness.

Basic Metabolic Rate (EMR)

Brain metabolism is directly related to body metabolism. One facet of the human body that the EEG will monitor is that of brain metabolism. Such gross metabolic dysfunctions as liver or kidney failure are easily seen with the EEG. Epilepsy is also seen as resulting in a metabolic dysfunction within the brain. Because of these and other important applications, the EEG was incorporated into the medical systems of Western society.

The EEG is also a good reflection of how well oxygen is metabolized in the blood. Your body needs oxygen in order to convert food resources into energy. Any deviation in oxygen intake and carbon dioxide output changes the EEG reading. Both hyperventilation and hypoventilation cause the EEG pattern to slow down. The amount of sugar, as a food resource, also affects the EEG.

Brain Activity and the Source of Alpha Waves

The EEG is considered to monitor "gross" neuronal activity. It does not monitor individual neurons per se, but large groupings. Whenever rhythms are seen in the EEG, it is the net result of many thousands of neurons "in unison."

Alpha is seen so easily with an EEG, and because of this, it was originally thought that there must be some kind of intra-cranial control mechanism, such as a biological pacemaker, caused all of those neurons to fire in unison.

Recently, two Dutch scientists claimed to have proven the existence of such an alpha-pacemaker. It, supposedly, was located in the thalamus, located in the brain stem. It was thought to "gate" (regulate/relegate) impulses from the body (spinal cord) into appropriate locations in the brain. Hand impulses are, thus, relegated into that part of the brain designated as hand. Alpha, then, was thought to be a very rhythmic relegating of the information from the body to the brain.

This rhythmic relegating, which results in alpha, is thought to be associated with a very relaxed state. Non-rhythmic relegating, resulting in dyssynchronous (CICR) brain wave activity, was considered a type of coping response, a response to impinging stimuli.

While the pacemaker theory of alpha is still tentative, it has not yet received wide recognition within the scientific community. This is a result of a very complex relationship between autonomic nervous system activity, brain metabolism, age, and a host of other pertinent factors.

Training Levels of Consciousness

One of the most important facets of the EEG is that it is an excellent indicator of levels and states of consciousness. Audio or visual inspection can determine whether a person is alert, relaxed, drowsy, asleep or even dreaming. Specific detail and arbitrary limit-points for various levels of consciousness are now defined by EEG parameters. The field of altered states of consciousness (ASC), and exploration and control of consciousness, are all a direct result of this very important tool.

It is often thought that through the introduction of these new tools, new techniques and discoveries can be made. The tremendous advances in electrons made in, and during, the past decade have advanced development of sophisticated equipment which stimulated psycho-physical research and new ideas in science. This is especially true in the areas of biofeedback and self-control technologies.

The technique of biofeedback is based on the fundamental process of instrument learning. A situation gives rise to several variable behaviors. One response is, in some way, rewarded or reinforced. Learning occurs as this response occurs successively more and more quickly and reliably. Essential to this learning process is the receiving of information in a feedback loop similar to servo systems. This can be done via visual or auditory stimuli which states when we have made the correct response or moved closer to our goal.

This is made possible by using electronic feedback loops (such as those provided by an Electro-encephalophone or EEP) and a psychological technique called operand conditioning. The first successful attempts were attributed to Joe Kamiya in the late 1950's. Essentially, his technique gave a signal when he achieved specific levels of consciousness. Its full potential has yet to be realized.

Behavior has traditionally been divided into two categories:

1. Voluntary control, such as walking, writing, muscular activities.

2. Autonomic control, such as heartbeat, blood pressure, brain wave production, body visceral processes.

We learn to guide behavior by receiving feedback on the results and then making appropriate adjustments. This is the place where the voluntary and involuntary behavior differs. While we can receive feedback in our writing, we do not have such access to receive feedback from the visceral activities. If provided with this absent feedback via electronic means, it has been shown conclusively that man can learn to exert a "voluntary" control over inner body functions.

Previous research into the control of heartbeat, blood pressure, body temperature, brain wave production and pain, has indicated that conscious controls of these internal states are possible. Subsequent research into control of brain waves through the use of biofeedback techniques has mostly centered on alpha waves, and more recently, theta.

In discussing biofeedback research and results, we run into a problem of semantics. It is the idea of learning to "control" our brain waves. It must be emphasized that in using these techniques, we are not learning to directly control the neuronal electrical activity of action potentials and synaptic events (in the cerebral cortex). We learn to control the subjective or mental events, associated with the presence of alpha or theta.

Changes in brain wave patterns, blood pressure, body-temperature, and deep muscle tension are "physiological" correlates of physiological processes that the subject learns to control.

Brain Wave Patterns

The pattern of neuronal activity in the cerebral cortical section of the brain can be recorded electrically. This is done by measuring the electrical potential difference between two points on the scalp. The record is known as the electroencephalogram (EEG). Brain waves manifest themselves as oscillating voltage. They have two main dimensions: the frequency of oscillation and the amplitude.

The frequency predominately determines the amplitude of the brain wave, but there can be fluctuations of amplitude at a given frequency. Brain waves are broken up into four main categories determined by the frequency of the wave. The borders of these categories are more or less arbitrary. The following table is approximately correct:

Gamma - This is a rarely achieved state of brain wave activity, quite toxic and dangerous with potential brain damage. It is not associated with better cognitive function. As such, only limited studies exist.

STATE	FREQUENCY (cps)	AMPLITUDE (microvolts)	COMMENT
Gamma	25 - 60	0.5 - 2	Hyper-aroused and quite dangerous to the brain
Beta	12 - 25	1 - 5	Conscious brain state. Fast dysnchronous activity
Alpha	8 - 12	20 - 80	Conscious brain state. Synchronous activity
Theta	4 - 8	5 - 10	Usually unconscious. Slow rhythmic activity
Delta	0.5 - 4	100 - 200	Usually unconscious. Very large rhythmic activity.

Beta - This is a conscious brain wave. It is characterized as a state of being awake, alert, and concentrating. If this stage is maintained for a prolonged period, it becomes associated with feelings of tension, worry, fear, or anxiety. Lower brain states (often associated with sleep and dream states) are necessary on an occasional basis to maintain the alert aspect of this state. This is the state where a visual-identification in our minds eye occurs, a state where images are identified with form and specific objects.

Alpha - This is also a conscious state, but identified with the mental experience where images are not identified. It has come to be associated with feelings of pleasure, pleasantness, tranquility, serenity and relaxation. It can also imply a relaxed concentration. It is also a place of light sleep and several dream states.

Theta - This state is traditionally labeled unconscious by Western medicine. In recent years, however, people trained with autogenics can achieve this state and retain consciousness, similar to Eastern meditation. Theta has come to be associated with such things as hypnagogic imagery, day dreaming, sleep, cognition of problem solving, future planning, remembering, switching thoughts, and creativity. It is also now been shown to be when maximum regeneration of cells occurs (self-healing).

Delta - This state is predominately associated with non-dreaming sleep or deep sleep. There are some reports of individuals achieving this set of brain wave patterns and still retaining consciousness. If it is achieved while maintaining a conscious state, "out-of-body" (OOBE) experiences are subjectively experienced and reported.

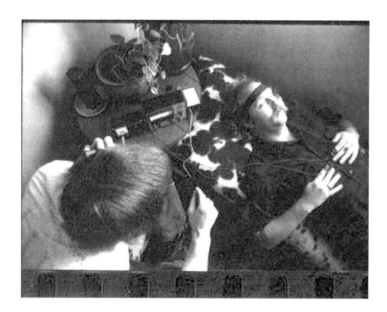

Normal Sleep Cycles

The EEG pattern changes throughout the night. These changes can determine when dreaming occurs. The chart below is an average sleep cycle during those eight hours.

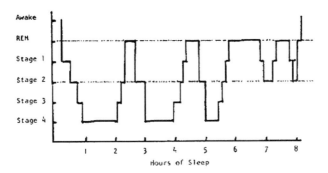

Stage 1 is the drowsy period of sleep characterized by what is known as sleep spindles (spindle-alpha).

Stage 2 is a sleep where responses to external and/or internal stimulation can occur. This stage is characterized by what are known as K-complex waves.

Stage 3 is when we are on our way down to State 4. It is a transition from Stage 2 to Stage 4 sleep, very short in period, and is associated with dream states.

Stage 4 is deep sleep. It is also delta state and is not associated with dreaming. The REM (Rapid Eye Movement) state is where most dreams occur.

Notice how we spend most of the first part of the night in Stage 4 sleep. The latter part of the night is spent mostly in REM sleep. Therefore, most dreams occur shortly before awakening. When this stage is deprived or not allowed to occur, temporary personality changes occur along with other psychological changes. When we make up that lost sleep, we will spend more of it in a lighter stage of REM. In a sense, this makes up for that lost dream time.

47

Although there is a lot of variable data on EEG changes with age, there is a basic curve that shows the usual rate of development and change with time. Primarily, the EEG frequency of a person stays very low. A newborn infant is about 1 o 2 cps. This gradually increases until the age of 19 when, while awake, the normal adult rhythm is about 20 cps.

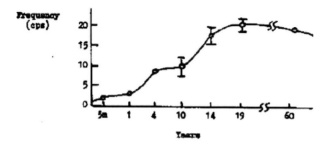

Things which lower the EEG frequency

LSD, sedative drugs

Large doses of alcohol

Very low blood sugar

Lack of oxygen

Things which raise the EEG frequency

Caffeine

Small doses of alcohol, barbiturates

Low blood sugar

Excess of carbon dioxide (CO_2)

Hypnosis (per se), has little effect on the EEG. It is what is contained in the hypnotic suggestion that changes brain frequencies and causes changes in brain wave states.

How an EEG Works

The EEG generates a feedback signal by picking up the very low voltage brain wave signals with two or more electrodes. A high-gain circuit amplifies the signal and drives a wide band filter. This filter passes signals in the alpha through delta range and attenuates signals of higher and lower frequencies. The feedback is usually in the form of a modulated white-noise with the modulation at the brain wave frequency. There are usually two controls, one for amplitude variations and the other to discriminate frequency bands (for tighter control).

The cerebral cortex is the outer most part of the brain. It is this convoluting mass of tissue that man has more of than any other animal. The cortex of each hemisphere is divided into four main areas called lobes. Alpha is found predominately on the occipital lobe or back-part of the brain. This is the section which deals with visual systems. Alpha is also found in the frontal lobe, but not as easily. Theta is found more commonly on the temporal lobe; whereas, speech and the sensory and motor areas of the brain tend to show primarily more beta activity.

Electrode placement usually uses a ground, or reference point, under one ear. The potential generated between the two electrodes is very important. Therefore, the second electrode is usually placed in the occipital region, to one side about one inch just under the inion (the "bump" found at the back of the skull). The side chosen is the same side that the "ear" electrode is on. This gives the easiest and optimum gradient form of brain signals being monitored.

Potential Application

Pleasure, relaxation and sleep are associated with alpha-theta output. The combination of relaxing, clearing the mind and turning inward can be a very pleasant and rewarding experience. Learning to relax and go from alpha to theta has proven to be beneficial to the insomniac. In some cases, it can also be a sleep-substitute.

Hypnosis patients are much more susceptible to suggestion when in lower alpha states. It is now possible, within several weeks of autogenic training, to achieve states of consciousness to those of Zen masters with 20 years meditation effort. The main drawback once we learn these states is that continual reinforcement is necessary for similar ability results.

One of the main purposes for sleep is to transfer information and experiences from short to long-term memory. Concentration, learning and recall ability can, and is, greatly enhanced with alpha-theta control exercises. Recall capability is greatest in alpha state. Also, by learning to exclude all external stimuli when trying to achieve alpha-theta control, we increase our ability to concentrate.

The reverie state, which is indicated by theta and low-frequency alpha, seems to increase hypnagogic and dream-like images. There is also a link between reverie and hypnagogic imagery and creativity. These images are critical for the creative process.

Other Biofeedback Systems

EMG (Electromyography) is used for hypertension, deep muscle control, and reading improvement by eliminating "sub-vocalization."

Thermal Feedback is used for controlling body temperature at various points on the body. Current research shows that most individuals can raise or lower finger temperatures about eight degrees Fahrenheit. This is also very useful in the control of migraine and tension headaches.

GSR (Galvanic Skin Response) is used as a lie detector and, supposedly, is a way of communicating with certain plants. Although the latter is highly questionable, there is a statistical significance in the change of skin resistance in certain fish eight hours prior to a major earthquake, offering a new early-warning system for the prediction of major quakes in high-risk areas.

These have been just a few of the many suggested possible applications. An exciting field with promise, biofeedback technique research should provide more new discoveries and ideas for years to come.

Video Feedback: Self Realization through Yogatronics

Biological feedback (bios means life and feedback meaning return to source) experimentation has been found to be particularly well-suited to the Western mind. The concept of time is much more important as everyone is in a hurry. Consequently, the western mind looks for "short-cuts" using technology. Research and experience has shown this technology to be a rapid and promising means toward such goals as self-awareness, health, and self-exploration.

Recent technological advances, such as biofeedback instruments, have enabled man to realize the potentials of his inner power. These include mental concentration for problem solving, appetite control, preventive medicine, training to control heart-rate, blood pressure, skin-temperature, anxiety, and other measureable body functions. Every day there are new examples of where this concept of technology enters our life. The state of this art has become very sophisticated. With currently technologies now standard in most homes, a technological transcendence is now available, similar to ancient Eastern experiences of Kundalini. Health and expanded mental capability would be by-products. The television can now be used to change habits, personality, weight and other characteristics while broadening our self-realization.

The application of biofeedback research to the everyday lives of people has many implications. These can range from mass brain washing to expanded consciousness for all mankind. By integrating several fields of study, advanced technology now provides new tools for achieving altered states of consciousness.

Populations can be re-programmed and individuals can become self-enlightened. An electronic meditation—using the most recently available information—is developed to create brain-body loops for interaction and control. The individual learns about the process of his own internal dialogue and can come to sense, and later manipulate, the loop of consciousness. Most of the hardware already exists in more and more homes.

Biofeedback Research

Changes in brain wave patterns, blood pressure, body temperature and/or deep muscle tension are "physiological" correlates of psychological processes that the subject learns to control. Some of the more outstanding developments in biofeedback research include the following examples:

Relaxation - Any degree of rapid, self-induced relaxation can be obtained by a number of biofeedback techniques. These include using muscle activity to operate the signals of an Electromyograph (EMG), even to the point of each individual muscle cell becoming relaxed.

Mental concentration for problem solving - The brain wave patterns which accompany effective, and efficient, mental activity are well-known. They are now used via Electroencephalograph (EEG).

Appetite control - When the compulsion to eat exists, the psychology and brain waves reflect this "drive state". We can train ourselves to recognize this state by paying attention to physiological signals. We can, then, train ourselves to distinguish between these signals and continue to reproduce a non-compulsive state.

Preventive medicine - The physiologic activity of each troublesome system can be used to "feedback" information about its own functioning. These include heart rate, blood pressure, respiration, skin temperature, gastric activity, intestinal motility, muscles and so on.

Training to control heart rate - The two major areas when using feedback techniques are as follows: (1) a wide variety of cardiac irregularities, particularly tachycardia, bracycardia, extra systoles and auricular flutter, and (2) psychological anxiety and fear reactions.

Training to control blood pressure - High blood pressure symptoms such as headaches and dizziness, and the more serious conditions resulting from high blood pressure, can be prevented when we have the ability to maintain our blood pressure. This can be life saving.

Training to control skin temperature in specific areas - This is an easy physiologic activity which we can learn to bring under control. Many disease processes involve constriction of the blood vessels in the hands, foot, or other body area causing pain and coldness. With feedback training, this vasoconstriction can be markedly reduced resulting in relief of both symptoms.

Anxiety - Numerous studies now indicate that a restful, relaxed, yet interested, subjective state is associated with alpha activity. Clinical emphasis is on assisting us to produce lower frequencies with higher amplitudes.

Education - Simple feedback systems are now used in conjunction with computer assisted teaching machines. It is well-known that the attention span of children is short. An accurate indicator of the length of each span of attention would be extremely useful in maximizing the use of teaching machines.

Drug use - Feedback techniques can increase the effectiveness of drug treatments. Since feedback techniques are applicable to all body systems, the can decrease intestinal contractions, lower blood pressure, and change skin temperature. They can also alleviate problems such as muscle tension, anxiety, irregular heartbeats, and respiratory distress. Undesirable side effects of the drugs can also be reduced.

Lie Detector - Some newer modifications with Galvanic Skin Response (GSR) have been used to determine stress potentials. The surface of the body does contain information about internal state functions; it is just a question of isolating variables.

Combined with video imagery received from a television screen, feedback becomes a means for human beings to experience a focused centeredness, not unlike trance states produced by Tibetan monks and other adepts.

Video Feedback

Video feedback is a continuously progressing feed-forward loop of light traveling through a video recording and projection system. It usually interfaces a

television camera and a television screen or monitor. Through the manipulation of the television camera it is possible to create, manipulate and define
video images.

Biofeedback involves the externalization of internal states and processes.
This permits easier manipulation of the process. Video feedback involves
the interlocking of internal and external loops. In effect, there are electronic
mandalas with great powers for focusing concentration, stimulating artistic
appreciation and altering conscious perception.

Electronics creates video mantras through mantra-tronics, yoga-tronics and
video light loops. Video systems detect patterns of energy at the camera and
then process these patterns and project them onto a screen. Video feedback
loops the screen back to the camera. Patterns arise which can grow brighter
(positive feedback), fainter or remain constant (negative feedback).

The next stage is to add the human brain and other autonomic functions into
the light loop. As the brain might act as the "camera," the signal sent to the
processor could also be altered in such a form as to "more efficiently" move
the brain into a previously determined state of awareness."

Today, video feedback has been only used to permit eye-hand manipulation
of the described interlocked loops. This, then, helps the individual to understand and manipulate his own inner loops (eye-hand) more easily. But, what
if we were to monitor brain waves? The signal could be "processed" and a
computer could, then, direct an "altered" signal to the screen monitor. This
"altered" pattern would be calculated to be the "most efficient" feedback in
assisting the brain to achieve the "desired state".

We are not talking about those auditory and visual cues we uses to single
out motor units and control their isolated construction. There are specific
patterns, colors and sounds which, in our selves, move us toward those predetermined states. With this in mind, the system for feedback would include:

Brain/body monitors/amplifier system - These signals then go to a gating system.

Gating system - This sets the threshold and level sense with timing parameters. The brain/body information is now ready to go to pattern recognition.

Pattern recognition (associative, memory, array) - These signals, then, go to a probabilistic synthesis control system.

Probabilistic synthesis control system - This has the ability to be pre-programmed for specific signal forms to the video/audio feedback devices.

Video/audio feedback devices - These deliver the "altered" stimuli to complete the loop. The new evoked responses are registered and the process begins anew.

The key is the probabilistic synthesis control system. It is here that the feedback loop system can be altered for specific goals or direction of meditation. In Florida, for example, several grade school systems use a brain-video feedback system. The children watch their lessons on TV. When their attention begins to wander, the individual brain patterns drop in frequency.

At a certain (predetermined) frequency, the lesson is stopped (by a computer) and a new stimulus is given to the child (usually an action scene, i.e. Western). This "snaps" the consciousness of the child back to "attentive" and the lesson is resumed. This simple form of video feedback in Education has improved reading and math skills 40-80% above norms. Imagine what advanced research in computer-graphics might yield.

Pattern Recognition

A primary function of the brain is in the recognition of patterns. This is the ability to perceive general inter-relationships between different parts of an input signal. These signals are usually visual, acoustical or tactile. It can also do this for ideas and concepts.

The perception of such unexpected relationships lies at the very heart of humor and creativity. The difficult part of pattern recognition is to see past the local variations into the pattern lying beneath. This is not a signal-to-noise ratio problem because the patterns beneath are not necessarily the same.

Recognition does not seem to be simply a matter of recall from a vast memory because we can distinguish patterns (like speech) without ever having heard them previously. Techniques like filtering, adaptation, correlation, and recollection are used today. The understanding of recognition is largely a matter of understanding how to deploy these various activities.

Equally important with pattern recognition is pattern synthesis. These are the techniques of generating the complex electric nerve signals which give rise to speech and coordinated muscle movement. The ability to speak or write reveals a genuine creative ability. In some sense, pattern synthesis is the converse of pattern recognition. The synthesis process must play an important role in the use of context in recognition.

Memory and its various functions complete the primary functions of the brain. There are three basic types of memory:

1. *Short-term* is responsible for the events of the last few seconds. It is very accurate. It involves the storage of the signal long enough to bring context to bear on the recognition process.

2. *Long-term* is used to recall knowledge we have acquired, events experienced and ideas from previous thoughts. It is associative in character and stores can not be addressed except by association. This means that some quality of the signal processing mechanism makes some signals more suitable for memorizing than others.

3. *Similarity function* store contains the signal processing algorithms. These are the acquired habits of thought. Once in storage, they become very difficult to erase (or change), but are very easy to ignore.

It is in the short-term and long-term memories that we remember "facts" and explicit techniques, while it is in the function-store that we either learn or know how to think. Other functions of the brain would include signal processing, learning and adaptation.

At the heart of the problem of pattern recognition is the concept of similarity. Since no two patterns are identical, the act of pattern recognition is the act of perceiving a degree of similarity between an observed pattern and that memory. This enables us to classify the new one. It is, therefore, critical to apprehend different kinds of similarity and a very important part of pattern recognition which involves selecting the appropriate similarity function.

Pattern recognition nearly always involves some form of iterative process before a firm decision is made. It is either necessary to solve simultaneous equations or to form a hypothesis of what the pattern must be (usually with highly inadequate data). If it is the latter, then it must be tested until it becomes more or less recognizable.

The importance of context in the process of pattern recognition is clear. The kind of similarity to look for in correlating two signals depends on context. A pattern is really nothing more than a feature in the context of other features. This decoding of signals, by the use of contextual information, is a vital part of all aspects of pattern recognition.

A Model for Pattern Recognition

The repeated pattern of iterative feedback loops reflects a further repeated pattern and demonstrates how signals are processed by the brain. As modeled, a pattern is nothing more than the inter-relationships of the sub-patterns comprising it and these sub-patterns are the inter-relationships of various features. Conversely, features are only recognizable in terms of their contexts (the patterns they comprise) and patterns are only recognizable in terms of their environment.

It is therefore expected that all aspects of pattern recognition are performed in the same system. The model proposed has three main iterative loops of which the signal analyzer, the similarity function and the addressing of the associative stores are optimum. Patterns, in general, differ not so much by some quantitative measure as by some qualitative dissimilarity, or quality of the pattern.

This type of system was first proposed by Hill in 1969 for a speech recognition machine:

1. The *analyzer* contains transducers and circuits which transform the signal into sequences of features.

2. The *associative store* should contain templates of feature sequences as well as templates of deep structure and class. The function is to bring contextual information to bear upon the recognition process. Correlation eliminates, or reduces errors, and plays a major role in synthesis.

3. The *comparator* is where the input feature sequences are organized into a form in which they can search the associative store for similar storage.

4. The *similarity function* store contains the algorithms specifying the various types of similarity and classes of patterns it can handle. If you wish the machine to learn, it is into this store that the new algorithms would be written, representing new points of view.

5. The *generalizer* is a higher level pattern recognizer in that it identifies similarities between classes. Via the store selector, it directs the search through the associative store to those parts of it which are most likely to contain the patterns sought.

Every computer, whose operation and structure is completely known, will consist of two independent systems, the hardware and the software. The hardware contains the memory, input, and output devices, and performs the actual work. The software provides the instructions for what to compute which, alone, determines the meaning of the computation.

For example, one could monitor the state of every computing element at all times and, in the case of a binary language, portray this by a table of zeros and ones as a function of time. However, without the knowledge of the software, such tabulation provides no clue to the meaning of what is being computed. The software, alone, determines the intelligence content of the computer output.

The Software

New research has demonstrated the capability of showing clear relationships between specific brain output patterns of a given artist and specific types of expressive, artistic activity. In addition, it has recently become possible to isolate aspects of the brain's evoked response to sensory stimuli, physical and imagined.

Clynes has shown that characteristic and highly repeatable response shapes or waveforms can be recorded from motor activity during the overt expression of a specific emotion or idea or during physical articulation of rhythmic pulses in music from a particular composer. He is a medical doctor working at the Research Center in Rockman State Hospital in Orangeburg, New York.

Recent and current research is showing that the brain's evoked response to a sensory stimulus can be broken down and analyzed in such a way as to relate specific peaks in the evoked response waveform to specific aspects of either the stimulus, itself, or the processing behavior of the participant. The evoked response is primarily dependent on two factors:

1. The physical parameters of the stimulus

2. The significance or meaning of the stimulus that is dependent on subjective experience.

E. Roy John, a pioneer in the understanding of the brain states:

> *"When an experienced organism receives a novel and meaningless stimulus and generalization occurs, this new afferent input in a familiar context activates the representational system in such a way as to cause release of a common mode of activity like that stored during the learning experience."*

and

> *"Analogous data from experiments with human beings indicate that phase-locked potentials are released at the time that absent stimuli are expected to occur. Furthermore, the wave-shapes released when particular visual stimuli are imagined resemble the wave-shapes of potentials evoked by actual presentation of the imagined stimuli."*

Clynes took a number of volunteers and shaved their heads, placing a series of electrodes in rosette patterns on various regions of the head. These included the temporal, frontal lobe section and occipital regions of the brain. In this way, not only were brain frequencies monitored, but directional shifts in these frequencies could also be determined by the geometry of the electrode configuration on the skull.

The original purpose of Clynes' work was to find how precision and order exist in brain processes. This was to discover what is inherently programmed in man and how he might make use of that inherent program.

These individuals were given a number of images (form) and colors to concentrate on while their brain was monitored by computers. Recording from opposite pairs of electrodes simultaneously, he obtained views of the electrical activity from different angles: mathematically, a spatial differentiation of the electrode vector. What he was mapping was consciousness (literal).

He, literally, mapped out the fields in the human brain. A computer then was able to identify and reproduce those geometrical figures the subject was concentrating (mind's eye), as a geometric form with color, so it could be recognized as a specific object. The subject did not even have to look at the pattern, but simply concentrate "in his mind's eye". A standing wave means that the wave is not changed, but is holding itself steady in one certain geometrical thought.

A number of very important observations were made:

1. Certain qualities and relationships were of greater importance to the computer than such quantitative factors such as intensity. This meant that the brain's system of identification is based on differences rather than intensity of the signal.

2. Thin lines were found to produce characteristic evoked potentials irrespective of size. The form, itself, is transduced into another form in the brain "space-time" which can be measured. There is a one-to-one correspondence between visual forms of the stimulus, the response forms in the brain, and the perception.

This is, perhaps, the first physical description of the field of an archetype. It is a geometrical structuring and has uniqueness.

3. The process of inhibition is as important for transducing the external world as is excitation. Concentration on specific lines of geometry does not constitute the changing stimulus, but their steady presence systematically, and radically, alters the response to another changing stimulus.

4. Changes in intensity of a single color produce very simple response shape. Light and darkness (as opposites) show no evidence of being different values of the same variable. Rather, they seem to be the result of stimulating and, also, of inhibiting different receptors. Thus, the evoked potentials to light and darkness in no way may be said to be positive and negative, respectively. White, for example, appears in this view as the result of mutual inhibition of color.

5. These experiments clearly imply an inherent form of organization and not a random learning of nerve nets. It is possible to mentally recognize and perceive the stimulus within the first portion of the evoked potential.

Responses (in the brain) which occur later than 0.3 seconds are seen as systematic processes, or tuned circuits, to those responses to specific in-coming stimuli. This is a form of resonance in the brain. They act like keys to "unlock" specific parts of our brain, often being observed below psychological threshold levels (subliminal).

Geometry and Archetypes

It is now evident that every stimulus corresponds to a particular "space-time" shape in the brain (in terms of electrical activity). A computer can even identify these shapes, much like "looking into someone's mind and seeing their pictures". These "space-time" shapes are evidence of relationships between the external world and its representation in the brain.

I have chosen to call these spatial-temporal representations "keys". These "keys" seem to operate on "locks" in our brain in a manner similar to the "minting" of DNA production and replication. An archetype may, then, be seen as a specific geometrical system of standing waves occurring in the brain as a "space-time" shape or "key".

In living organisms, opposites receive their structuring of symmetry from particular combinations of spatial and temporal aspects. Like the reins on a horse, each of the opposites of the physiological pair has its own place. While they do balance motion, in themselves, they do not cancel each other.

This geometric aspect makes them capable of being opposites. The activity of each arm determines the quantity of the turn; the spatial identity of the rein determines the quality. There is no monotonic (or linear) transition from one to the other passing through some form of "zero".

Information is embodied in a field rather than just being a field. The geometrical images are, basically, an abstract quantity of information; a field relationship between one point and another in the universe. Unlike most engineering channels of communication, biological channels are dynamically asymmetric. Information on change is transmitted across space asymmetrically with respect to the direction of the change of the variable.

This means that if a biological system is to be informed symmetrically about dynamic changes, it requires two channels. The basic reason for this dynamic asymmetry is that biological channels for control use the concentration of molecules to transmit information at some point along the channel. This must involve an asymmetry since the creation and transportation of molecules is, generally, accomplished by different means from their breakdown and removal.

Concentration can be made a function of information as long as the change requires an increase in concentration. Decreasing concentration, generally, cannot be accomplished as fast through the same channel. The level of hormones, which have issued into the bloodstream, cannot be decreased through the action of the same gland.

A decrease in concentration is produced by metabolic processes or through the increase in level of a counteracting hormone or chemical. In either case, the decrease in concentration is produced through quite different channels from the one producing an increase in concentration.

The significance of this asymmetry of uni-directional rate sensitivity in the "space-time" patterns in the brain is that, if it were not for this principle, interaction and cancellation of opposites would prevent the formation of unique "space-time" patterns for each perception. In this case, memory could become impossible (as defined).

An event is registered as a pattern in space as well as a pattern in time. With the sense of touch, for example, removal does not cancel the sensation, even when the touch was short and momentary. Thus, a distinction can be made between quality and quantity. Quality is given by the channel location and quantity by the firing pattern in the channel.

In living organisms, opposites receive their structure of symmetry from a particular combination of spatial and temporal aspects. It is the geometric properties which makes them capable of being opposites. This "rein control" implies distinction between quality and quantity. With each rein, messages are similar and not opposite in character. The activity of each "rein" determines the quantity; the spatial identity of the "rein" determines the quality.

Any view of the universe is an interplay between information and energy. Information stands for those processes which provide recognition and identification of separate existences. Energy stands for the transformation and displacement of the contents of space. This interplay between information and energy involves identity, quality and recognition.

The Vector Equilibrium Matrix

The use of geometry and geometrical forms as video tools offers intriguing possibilities. They allow experiential interaction with archetypes or god-forms. They also grant access to those specific altered states where one experiences the eternal aspect of sacred time: A consciousness of immortality.

A geometrical image is developed in the book *The Diamond Body: A Modern Alchemical View of the Philosopher's Stone.* This image comes from the field of solid state physics, corresponding to both the Jewish mystical traditions and current concepts in imaginal psychology. A mathematical model is generated to assist the development of anima consciousness via a visualization exercise called *The Diamond Body Exercise,* (DBE).

A series of biological resonances occur between specific internal-state functions and the "outside". These resonance relationships are discussed, and specific models are given, to aid visualization and resonance. This practice of meditation develops a common ground, uniting psyche with matter. Through the stabilization and equilibrium fostered in the individual during meditation sessions, the individual is brought into increased harmony with the environment.

More importantly, a "repair function" is now available which reverses those entropic functions related to libido.

The DBE is a breakthrough in meditation techniques. Steeped in mystery, the *Merkabah* Chariot of *Sephir-Yetzirah*, Ezekiel's vision and *"the Cube of Space"* is all the same thing. It is a regeneration meditation for immortality. And, it is now available to the common household....

It is the contention of this book that the most fundamental (pre)geometric form is the *Vector Equilibrium Matrix* (VEM). The vector equilibrium construct, first proposed by Buckminster Fuller, describes the most economical lines of movement within the atomic nucleus. This geometry form leads directly to the *Diamond Body of the Cube of Space.*

To place oneself inside this structure, or to project this matrix form outward as a visualization, creates and generates a resonance within the "space-time" shapes of the brain. *The Vector Equilibrium Matrix* is a geometrical Mandela resonating with the psychological analog for the Philosopher's Stone!

The *Vector Equilibrium Matrix* is a visual tool which connects macroscopic structures to quantum modes. It graphically depicts the sphere, whose center is everywhere, and whose circumference is nowhere. It can be used as an access tool for realizing multiple quantum ordering.

To begin to understand this form of order, a new tool for perception is needed. The new concepts of order involve the discrimination of the relative differences in "space-time" (and similarities). Attention should now be given to *similar differences* and *different similarities*. Such a format in mathematics is called a ratio, or matrix field. *"The universe is a cosmic computer on the pre-geometric level of information in which space and time appear as secondary statistical constructs."*

The Vector Equilibrium Matrix is such a matrix field. Although seen as a geometry at any stage; it is pre-geometric in that it describes the change from one stage to the next. It is a quantized state of information.

A video projection of this Diamond Body structure is now possible with rotation of axis and "rising on the planes" (from spherical coordinates). The resulting geometries create specific "space-time" patterns in the brain. The resulting patterns allow "access" to those specific archetypes (associated with specific "space-time" patterns). They are known as "*Star Gates*" or "planetary gates" in mystical literature.

Real-Time Color Graphics

Most problems in complex structure and function require visualization. And, as the size of the structure increases (like "rising on the planes"); a third dimension is needed to give visualization perspective (context).

Real-time color graphics systems have unique advantages for the display of information. Studies of the structures and interactions of large biological molecules require both coordinate data and three-dimensional visualization. Software has been developed that now allows real-time display of color line and surface displays. Now that we have hardware and software for selective display of complex objects in color and stereo with real-time rotation, depth cueing, and interaction, another program is underway to insert the *Vector Equilibrium Matrix* into this program for use in a video feedback system.

This real-time color graphics system would respond to logic circuitry in the *similarity function store*. The feedback from the video section would bring up an iteration loop, going from the "space-time" patterns in the brain to the television. A rotation or depth cueing ("rising on the planes") would create a similar (and very specific) corresponding change in the "space-time" pattern.

> *Most importantly, this could be done as a pre-programmed response directing our brain to specifically desired "experiences" or archetypal encounters.*

Considerations in Design

A general purpose bio-medical preamplifier should form the front end of any comprehensive system. Accurate frequency discriminations (2-20 Hz), and the feedback system, should be capable of responding to peaks or zero crossing of in-band signal oscillations. It must be able to change in signal amplitude.

This means that a good variable threshold detector and envelope follower should be included in the over-all system. The input section should be capable of either AC or DC coupling, depending on specific applications, and provide a choice of fixed gain of about 3 or variable gain of about 5. Other measures, such as time spent producing the desired signal, are useful, but more expensive. They are, also, less likely to be needed.

The major sources of error are those due to biological sources, electrodes, amplifier, interaction between the amplifier and sources, filtering techniques, and detection circuitry. For example, as EEG signals are among the smallest recordable through gross methods, they are the most plagued by "leakage" from muscle potentials (EKG signals).

Thus, it is necessary to use differential amplifying techniques in order to obtain accurate results, subtracting a background signal which is a common problem between closely placed electrodes. Other factors presenting problems are the high impedance of biological sources such as 100K ohms, or higher, on the skin. The body is, also, a rather good radio/TV antenna, picking up unpredictable DC noise.

Complete designs for comprehensive biological monitoring/feedback units are described by Rosenboom. He, and a number of other artists, built these units to drive electronic synthesizers and color organs in the early 1970's. They were, essentially, creating "alpha-concerts". A number of shows were performed and the specific logic and hardware is outlined in his book. There is even a design for an *Evoked Response Peak Detector* by R. Koehler in this volume.

Summary

With existing technologies in hardware/software, it is now possible to use the home computer/television as a very powerful tool where health and expanded mental capabilities are only by-products.

A new dimension of learning and self-realization is available for the home. Biofeedback research has advanced the fields of medicine and health. It is, now, possible to control and direct specific autonomic functions which were, previously, not available or semi- control over a ten year yoga program. Video feedback systems are, now, successfully used in learning/education programs.

New models on pattern recognition and the nature of information nets allow for simple models which could be used with home computers (large memory).

The research of Clynes and Hill shows a clear relationship between specific brain output patterns and *specific* geometry. A first state for describing the physical analogs to unique archetypes is developed. Specific geometrical images will invoke specific brain responses.

A formula emerges. *The Vector Equilibrium Matrix* is a visual tool which connects (or describes) the change from one state to another. It is the method in which a specific "space-time" pattern changes into another with uniqueness. This matrix has already been set into a grid of values and qualities based on Jewish mystical traditions and current concepts in imaginal psychology.

A mathematical model is generated to assist the development of anima consciousness via a visualization exercise called *The Diamond Body Exercise*. A video projection of this Diamond Body structure is, now, possible in the home. The resulting effects lead to the possibility of pre-programmed response, directing our brain to specifically desired "experiences" or archetypal encounters.

Previous designs for biofeedback systems, using audio and visual, are described. The immediate applications for the use of these systems in the home are staggering. Populations can be re-programmed and individuals can become self-enlightened. Electronic meditation creates brain-body loops for interaction and control. This state of control is a form of technological transcendence. On the mundane level, this proposed system could be used to loose weight, stop smoking and change other deep habits.

Conclusions

There is obviously a very immediate need for research. The implications of this range from mass brain washing to expanded consciousness for all of mankind. Approximately 95% of the households in the United States have at least one television set. Home computers will match this percent within another ten.

The design problems for this type of system are minimal. Hardware, now, exists in a variety of markets and is competitive. The installation is also simple, plugging RF inputs to the antenna leads of any TV system. All bio-monitoring equipment is similarly fashioned to the body with some form of isolation (optical). They, probably, will be available within five years through such game systems as Odyssey or Atari.

The next advance will be a brain switch via neuro-electronic correlates. Already, there is known to be another "sensory motor" in-put in the microwave region (0.3-3.0 GHz). A feature called *Contingent Negative Variation* (CNC) has been isolated as a facet of the EEG through computer Fourier analysis and, somehow, corresponds to will. The two are related, somehow, but how is not known. Chapter 8 deals with this CNV in more detail.

CNV relates to the cessation of neutral scanning when an object or event is recognized. An individual could learn to trigger the appearance of the CNV even without the presence of any object. It is conceivable that this "switch" could trigger an implanted brain-terminal to some central computer. Data transmission might be via direct brain communication in this microwave region.

The other side of this technological advance is that unscrupulous advertiser might attempt to sell his products via subliminal geometrical/color patterns in his advertisements. Since most of us do not have conscious awareness of this new sense, these unscrupulous messages would, automatically, be submerged into our consciousness. If this is true, and it does in fact appear so, then one country could conceivably broadcast specific microwave patterns toward their neighbor to, somehow, affect the social or group consciousness.

It appears as if, with all other "breakthroughs", it is a double-edged blade. Using this type of system, the future could show changes in the "school" concept is changed, and classes taking place at home. Currently, only 10% of the cerebral cortex is used, but a major jump in this percentage will occur with use and access to this concept of learning.

It is quite conceivable that the future will also allow for new concepts in our relationship to "time" and "space". Uniting psyche with matter has always been associated with immortality:

"To practice the ecology of the soul is to recycle one's consciousness"

VIDURU TELEMAHANDI — THE CHURCH OF SELF-AMPLIFICATION

Some Further Resources

Bohm, David: *Wholeness and the Implicate Order*, London,
          Rutledge & Kegan Paul, 1980.

Clynes, M. and Milsum, J. (ed.) *Biomedical Engineering Systems*, Chapter 7:
          "Toward A View of Man", McGraw-Hill Books, N.Y., 1970.

Frey, Allen N.:"*Human Perception of Illumination with Pulsed Ultrahigh
          Frequency Electromagnetic Energy*", Science, Vol.181, July 1973,
          pp556-8.

Fuller, Buckminster *Synergies 2*, Macmillan Pub., NY (1979).

Hill, D.R. (1969) *An ESOTerIC approach to some problems in automatic
          speech recognition.* Int. J. Man-Machine Studies, 1, 101.

John, E.R."*Switchboard Verses Statistical Theories of Learning and Memory*",
          Science, Vol. 177, No. 4052, 1972.

Langridge, R., et al "*Real-Time Color Graphics in Studies of Molecular
          Interactions*", Science, Vol. 211, No. 13, Feb. 1981, pp 661-666.

Rosenboom, David (ed.)*Biofeedback and the Arts: Results of Early
          Experiments*, A.R.C. Publications, Vancouver, Canada, 1976.

3

INTELLECT

AIR TRIGRAM

HISTORIC CONTEXT—*In the early 1970s Bruce Lee was only just beginning to demonstrate the concept of* martial arts. *Back then such forms as* Tai Chi *were only considered a form of meditation. The military approached* jujutsu *as "an art of weaponless fighting employing holds, throws and paralyzing blows to subdue or disable an opponent."*

This definition was incomplete, and it was then realized that something more *was going on. Now called* the art of flexible adaptation, *the importance of breath control became a primary interest of study for the military. It represented the synchronizing of internal states with physical actions, which led to* enhanced *abilities in martial arts.*

The historic context is about seeing the importance of Air in enhancing movement with the body. To be able to chant in such a way as to create a change in the physical world (cymatics) was a way to have confirmation of our physical action from thought.

Chapter Three

Breath Control &
Virtual Audio

*Breath is the bridge which connects life to consciousness, which unites your body
to your thoughts.*

—THICH NHAT HANH

Breath Control

The control of breath is, perhaps, one of the single most important aspects of
good health. It is the first, and last, thing we do when we enter and exit life.
Yet, many of us take it for granted, allowing it to, often, dictate our behavior
and experience of life. In order to take more control of our life, we need to
learn how to move it from an automatic response into one dictated by the
parasympathetic nervous system. It also helps to relax us and slow us down.

Learning to Walk: This takes practice and often, may take years to achieve.
Tai Chi is, perhaps, one of the more disciplined exercises for this switch from
automatic to controlled responses. The most important aspect of Tai Chi is
how to breathe and walk. The two are the same when done as a foundation.
As we walk in normal life, if we imagine we are on a high-wire, we will show
uncertainty and rough balance. The fear from imagination is enough to challenge and disrupt our sense of balance.

Balance is a quality from breathing correctly and the sense of safety. There-fore, before we attempt o do the more complex movements in Tai Chi, we need to learn the correct breathing from the basic walk. The two, the breathing and the walk, become one and the same. After this, more complex movement can be achieved as there is balance and an absence of fear.

Once these two become one, with practice and time, the result becomes a type of muscle memory arbitrary to the perception. While balance gives us control of fear (and space), it is breath that controls our perception time. One way to see something as it truly is, is to forget how it was, then see it, again, as if it were for the first time. This is a Life Lesson.

When I began my Tai Chi lessons, my Chen Buddhist Sefu decided not to teach me any of the eight movements until I first learned how to walk. I had come from more than 12 years of study in hard-forms (Shoulin Buddhism). For one year, that is all I did. I learned how to walk and breathe as a symbol of one becoming another.

One day (almost one year later), he pulled me aside and offered to teach me the various eight movements of Tai Chi. His instruction, concerning movements, was to "you follow me." I had more than one year of watching his form, so I began to duplicate his form. We did this for almost ten minutes when he began to change his form. As a dedicated student, I never questioned his motives.

At that moment, something remarkable happened. While I followed his vari-ous movements, I noticed that I was, now, moving very fast, like a form of Hung Gou (Kung Fu). But, my experience of time was that all of our actions were in slow motion, like most are with Tai Chi.

Control of breath can (over time) allow us to change our perception of time. With that, our precision of movement becomes enhanced beyond normal or-dinary life experiences. At some level, we do this all the time. However, we do not really notice those changes, as we also record our experiences in chunks or units of time (duration).

On the Nature of Chi:

He who teaches without enlightenment kills the Buddha.

OLD ORIENTAL SAYING

It would be remiss if I did not mention more about the nature of Qi (Chi). The keys to regulating the breath and transporting Qi (energy) are in two places. The first, known as the *Huiyin* cavity, is located between the genitals and anus. The second is the palate of the mouth.

When the *Huiyin* cavity is pushed out, Qi, in the Yin vessels, is released. When it is lifted upward, the Qi is contained and condensed. As an example, when we laugh out loud, our exhalation is longer in duration than our inhalation. When we exhale, the *Huiyin* is pushed out naturally and the entire body's Yang is manifested. This strengthens the Guardian Qi. This makes the body warmer and, then, causes the body to sweat.

However, when sad or depressed, the inhalation is longer than the exhalation. The *Huiyin* is, then, lifted upward naturally and the Marrow Qi is increased. The Guardian Qi is, then, condensed inward and the body feels cooler. Coordinating the breathing with the *Huiyin* 's lifting and pushing is one of the key knacks to governing the entire body's Qi status.

In the past, it was common that a master would keep these two secret keys of self-regulation to himself. These secrets would not be revealed to the student until he/she proved trustworthy. They were not passed down to those disciples who were not loyal and moral.

One of the secret keys is learning how to control the *Huiyin* (perineum). This place is the controlling gate of the body's Yin and Yang. In Chinese, *Huiyin* means "meet Yin." It is also known as the meeting place of the four Yin vessels:

Conception (*Ren Mai*)
Thrusting (*Chong Mai*)
Yin Heel (*Yinqiao Mai*)
Yin Linking Vessels (*Yinwei Mai*)

When this gate is pushed out, the Qi in these four Yin vessels is released. When this gate is held up, the Qi in the four Yin vessels is kept in and preserved. These movements allow this gate to control the body's Yin-Yang status. This place acts as a pump (or piston) to a Qi chamber that controls the storage and release of Qi.

The other key is the palate of the mouth. Taoists believe that the palate is the connecting place of the Conception and Governing Vessels. Normally, the palate is not connected to the tip of the tongue and, therefore, the Qi is stagnant at the throat area for uttering sound.

Due to this stagnation (Qi), the mouth is dry. The Conception and Governing Vessels are not well connected in the mouth area. However, if we practice our martial art, or Qigong, without the necessity of making a sound, then we should touch our tongue upward to the palate, at all times, so as to connect the Conception and Governing Vessels.

When we do this, the root of the tongue will generate saliva to moisturize the throat and to calm down the Yang fire. This allows the Qi to be transported between these two main Qi Vessels without stagnation. This is what is called "releasing the heavenly water." This tongue connection is also known as "building the magpie bridge" (*Da Que Qiao*).

According to a Chinese story, long ago a Cowherd (*Niu Lang*) and a Weaving Maid (*Zhi Nu*) would meet once a year on the seventh day of the seventh moon on a bridge across the Milky Way. The bridge was formed by sympathetic magpies. This story has become a symbol of Yin and Yang's interacting, or connecting, in Qigong practice.

When Yin and Yang meet, the body can then be in harmony.

When the saliva is generated to a comfortable amount, you should swallow it and use the mind to lead it down to the real *Dan Tian*. This will help us lead the fire Qi downward to cool down the body.

If those who are learning *Taiji* can apply the above two keys into their regular natural breathing, then the accomplishment of *Taiji* Qigong can be achieved within days. At the beginning, it is hard to control our *Huiyin* 's movement smoothly and naturally. In addition, due to the positioning of the tongue, an uncomfortable and tense feeling may be experienced at the root of the tongue.

However, after we practice for some time, it become easier and more comfortable and internal practice will be more efficient and beneficial.

Normal Abdominal Breathing Instructions

Inhale slowly, deeply and quietly. As you inhale, expand the belly and gently push down the pelvic floor, or perineum. Then, exhale slowly, deeply, quietly, and draw in the belly, gently lifting the pelvic floor.

Hold the mind in the center of the belly. Energy follows consciousness. The Yi leads the Qi. Also, hold the mind in the center of your head between your two ears. Try to reside in both places simultaneously.

It is recommended to continue with this breathing for six months before moving into reverse abdominal breathing. During this first six months, *Dan Tian*s (lower abdomen) should definitely be felt.

Men, having trouble with this exercise, should try abstaining from sexual activity for several weeks. This changes the level of Qi faster than any other method. Once we have done this once or twice, Qi status will be more easily recognized. By building the habit of conserving Qi, sex will not affect Qi status as much.

Remember, it is always good to 'start over', even if you've moved on from normal abdominal breathing (NAB) to other breathing techniques because, when go 'back,' NAB will be experienced on another level...

Scuba Diving

Breathing seems simple, yet it has more impact on diving pleasure and safety than any other aspect of scuba training. Breathing is the only skill performed continuously throughout in-water activities. It controls becoming and staying relaxed and the ability to react to stress appropriately. Efficient breathing is the key to avoiding panic. How we breathe affects our buoyancy and level of exertion. It is, often, the limiting factor in the amount of time spent on a dive.

Although divers are, often, admonished to "breathe normally," the most effective breathing pattern for diving is not "normal" for most of us. On land, breathing is usually slow, shallow, and through the nose. Occasionally, we even hold our breath when in thought or straining. (We can test this by pressing your palms together hard and noting your breathing. For diving, we learn a different pattern that serves us better underwater. We breathe continuously, slowly, deeply, and through the mouth.

Our respiratory cycle begins when we inhale. Air passes through the nose and mouth and through the airway (trachea) which splits into two bronchial tubes. Each bronchial tube enters a lung, where it divides into progressively smaller bronchiole. These continue to branch until they reach the alveoli — the millions of microscopic air sacs through which our lungs exchange gases with the circulatory system. Each air sac is surrounded by a network of tiny blood vessels or capillaries.

The air we breathe on land, and out of a standard scuba tank, is composed of 20 percent oxygen, 79 percent nitrogen, and one percent carbon dioxide and other trace gases. A portion of the oxygen, in the inspired air, goes into solution in our blood by diffusing across the extremely thin membrane separating the alveoli and the capillaries. The oxygenated blood is, then, carried to the heart, where it is pumped through the arteries to all the body's tissues.

When the oxygen-rich blood reaches the body's cells via the arterial capillaries, each cell takes some oxygen and metabolizes it to produce energy. Carbon dioxide — a by-product of this metabolism — moves from the cells into the blood-stream, where it is carried by the veins back to the lungs. There, the carbon dioxide is diffused into the alveoli.

The air in the lungs now contains more carbon dioxide than oxygen, and it's exhaled from the body. Most people are surprised to learn that it is this buildup of carbon dioxide, not the decrease in oxygen, which is the primary stimulus to breathe.

The respiratory cycle is significant in scuba diving because our lungs were not designed to function underwater. Physical differences in the underwater environment, such as increased ambient (surrounding) pressure and the necessity to breathe through scuba equipment, decrease the efficiency of the air exchange process.

In addition, there are diver-controlled factors: the increased demand for oxygen placed on the body by moving through the water and the physical and psychological stresses of functioning in a foreign environment. Using the proper diving breathing pattern enhances our comfort and safety by maximizing the amount of air exchanged and the time it spends within our system.

Always breathe continuously. This is the most important safety rule in scuba diving. We are breathing air at increased pressure. As we descend, our air spaces are compressed, and as we ascend, they expand. To avoid serious injury and discomfort when diving, we equalize the pressure in our lungs, ears, and sinuses.

Health Benefits

Learning to breathe continuously seems simple enough but, all mammals, including humans, are born with the instinct to inhale and hold their breath when their face hits the water. We have all had water splashed in our face unexpectedly, right? If we react normally, we automatically hold our breath.

The first step in making breathing a learned skill is to become aware of it, to convert breathing from an automatic to a conscious act. A good example is learning to exhale whenever the regulator is out of our mouth. Since we can't inhale with the regulator removed, and it's dangerous to hold our breath, the only choice is to exhale. This keeps the airway open and the lungs safe from overexpansion. Yet, many students find it difficult to remember to exhale because it goes against instinct.

The pattern of slow, comfortable inhalation followed by slow, full exhalation is analogous to breathing patterns used in various types of relaxation techniques such a yoga and Lamaze birth training. This pattern, also, helps calm anxious divers.

Make it a habit to breathe consciously. Conscious breathing is the single most beneficial things we can do for our health. In order to understand the importance of breathing for health, let us review the physiological functions of breathing.

Dharma Singh Khalsa, M.D., provides an excellent account of the breath physiology in Meditation as Medicine. According to Dr. Khalsa, automatic breathing is often quite ineffective. Unfortunately, most of us tend to be limited to automatic breathing.

One third of us do not breathe well enough to sustain health. Oxygen intake and elimination of carbon dioxide is too inadequate to allow optimal functioning of the heart, liver, intestines and other vital organs.

Effects of Breath Control:

Cellular level - Longevity and health of every single cell in the body and brain depend on oxygen intake through breathing.

Nervous system - Conscious breathing, deep and slow, tones the entire central and peripheral nervous system.

Circulatory System - The quality and efficiency of blood circulation depends on breathing. When tiny air sacs in the lungs receive more oxygen, the heart pumps more blood into the body. The body, then, absorbs nutrients more effectively. Toxins and wastes are more thoroughly eliminated. Because breathing is so directly and closely linked with circulation, the diaphragm is, sometimes, referred to as the "second heart."

Muscles - Muscles are developed, or wasted, depending on the efficiency of breathing and blood circulation. When muscles do not get enough oxygen, they hurt.

Liver function - When breathing is shallow or irregular, the liver cannot adequately transmit the blood to the heart. Accumulated blood in the liver can cause inflammation. However, deep, slow and conscious breathing can suck up excess blood accumulated in the liver.

Digestive function - Khalsa observes that poor digestion, including heartburn, is one of the most common reactions to shallow breathing. Deep and slow breathing provides more blood to the alimentary canal, improves digestion, and reduces acidity and gas.

"Rotto-Rooter" function - Conscious breathing helps the lungs by cleansing them of the toxins and noxious waste. Inefficient lungs may retain all kinds of toxins, pollutants, allergens, viruses and bacteria. Deep and full breaths recruit the entire lung into the act and can clean it of noxious substances.

Mood Management - When the brain does not get enough oxygen, we feel anxious, dizzy or lightheaded. With an abundant supply of oxygen, we tend to feel energetic and cheerful. One of the best ways to calm ourselves is to breathe deeply.

Emphysema - Many people with emphysema suffer from anxiety and/or depression. Since the breathing has a direct effect on emotions, it appears that compromised breathing, as in emphysema, may contribute to such negative emotional outcomes. For those with emphysema, conscious breathing helps to maintain a positive mental attitude in spite of the illness. Conscious breathing and positive mental attitude aid each other by forming a virtuous cycle.

Immune Function - As the controlled breathing reduces stress and negative emotions, our immune function, too, may improve. According to Dr. Khalsa, conscious deep breathing can prevent respiratory infections including common colds. I have not had a common cold in the last couple of years, thanks to the continuous practice of deliberate deep breathing.

Pain Management - Deep, relaxing breaths, and the practice of consciously holding and releasing of breath, increases the production of endorphins which, in turn, reduce the feeling of pain.

Circular Breathing

Circular breathing is a technique used by players of some special wind instruments. It is used to produce a continuous tone without break. This is accomplished by breathing in through the nose while blowing through the mouth. This is done by storing air in the cheeks.

This technique is used extensively in playing the Australian didgeridoo, the Sardinian launeddas and Egyptian arghul. Other traditions include oboes and flutes of Asia and the Middle East. And now, a few jazz and classical wind players, also, utilize some form of circular breathing.

While attending a concert last year at The Britt Festival, Kenny G. came onto the stage via a side entrance for the audience. He walked toward the stage, amongst many listeners, while playing a single note for more than 10 minutes. He is perhaps, the world's most famous circular breather, setting a world record for holding a single note for 45 minutes.

The person inhales fully and begins to exhale and blow. When the lungs are nearly empty, the last volume of air is blown into the mouth, and the cheeks are inflated with this air. Then, while still blowing this last bit of air out by allowing the cheeks to deflate, the person must very quickly fill the lungs by inhaling through the nose prior to running out of the air in the mouth. If done correctly, by the time the air in the mouth is nearly exhausted, the person can begin to exhale from the lungs once more, ready to repeat the process again.

Physiologically, the process is similar to drinking at a water fountain and taking a breath of air while water remains in the mouth, without raising the head from the water stream. The body "knows" to not allow water into the lungs. It is this same instinct that a circular breather uses to play their instrument.

The didgeridoo is a wind instrument of Aborigines of northern Australia. It is, sometimes, described as a natural wooden trumpet or "drone pipe". Musicians, now, classify it as an aerophone. There are no reliable sources stating the didgeridoo's exact age, though it is commonly claimed to be the world's oldest wind instrument.

A didgeridoo is usually cylindrical, or conical, in shape and can measure anywhere from 1 to 2 meters in length, with most instruments measuring around 1.2 meters. Instruments shorter, or longer, than this are less common. Generally, the longer the instrument, the lower the pitch or key of the instrument. Keys from D to F are the preferred pitch of traditional aboriginal players.

This is another important form of breath control which is part of the process of creating more Chi in the body. Since Chi is associated with breath control and the ability to change time, this tool can teach where the altered state of consciousness is best centered for the higher forms of Chi. Chi is just another resolution in the hologram where the control of breath allows more energy toward a specific purpose.

Virtual Audio

Sound is another level of the hologram for breath, although it, also, impacts brain responses and other autonomic function with more detail. To use this technology to, somehow, create an environment for behavior and responses has now become an important power tool for use in the evolution of consciousness. Virtual Audio is sound that is specially processed to contain significant psycho-acoustic information to alter human perception into believing that the sound is actually occurring in the physical reality of three-dimensional space.

Virtual Audio is a new process of encoding audio in three dimensions, passively or interactively. It requires no special decoding equipment and provides a very accurate model of our hearing process. Virtual Audio is so accurate that the listener cannot distinguish Virtual Audio recorded sound from reality. Playback can be experienced on stereo, surround speakers, or standard headphones.

The Selective Hearing Process

In the field of audio, the selective hearing process is fundamental to stress-relief. The selective hearing process in the human auditory system is the ability of the brain to tune into audio cues and tune out unwanted audio cues in the listener's environment. Selective hearing means listening only to audio cues that the listener wants to hear and not to those he does not want to hear, all at the same time.

"The cocktail effect" is a selective hearing process that can be experienced, either, consciously or through subliminal cues. When recording with normal recording technology, the selective hearing process is lost. The human brain can no longer selectively hear. The brain will try very hard to distinguish individual audio cues, or try to break down the basic components of the audio cues, but will be unsuccessful.

Normal recording methods do not encode the three-dimensional spatial cues necessary for the brain to carry out the selective hearing process. The brain will be unable to pull apart, or selectively hear, different component audio cues. The exception is, then, if the volume of a specific audio cue is very loud, the brain will then be able to perceive the louder sound. Cues that are the same approximate volume will all blend in together.

Since the brain is trying very hard to decipher different sounds unsuccessfully, a type of stress is induced. The medium of standard audio technology, itself, actually induces stress. This stress will inhibit the listener from being emotionally involved with the audio cues optimally. With the use of Virtual Audio, the natural phenomenon of selective hearing is retained in the recording process.

Numerous audio cues that are moving in a sound field, which has been recorded using normal audio recording techniques, can become confusing to the brain since the listener cannot selectively hear specific sounds. When using Virtual Audio technology, the listener can selectively hear many sounds, stationary or moving, without confusion. Sound encoded in Virtual Audio protocols enable the human brain to do what it normally does in nature: to selectively hear various component audio cues in the listening environment.

Virtual Audio encoded material, inherently, contains much more information to be processed by the human brain than normal audio. The result is greatly enhanced communication and emotional response from the recording when using Virtual Audio technology. When recording sounds of nature or music, the use of this process is very important and, in fact, fundamentally necessary for relaxation, meditation and the relief of stress.

The Physics of Virtual Audio

When sound waves arrive at the head, they are modified acoustically in a directionally dependent manner by diffractive effects around the head. In virtual audio systems this is done by interaction with the outer ears, described by the *head-related transfer function* (HRTF).

A head-related transfer function (HRTF) is a response that characterizes how an ear receives a sound from a point in space; two ears can produce a pair of HRTFs which can be used to synthesize a binaural sound that seems to come from a particular point in space. It is a transfer function, describing how a sound from a specific point will arrive at the ear (generally at the outer end of the auditory canal).

While we have only two ears, we can locate sounds in three dimensions – in range (distance), in direction above and below, in front and to the rear, as well as to either side. This is possible because the brain, inner ear and the external ears work together to make inferences about location.

This ability to localize sound sources may have developed in humans as an evolutionary necessity, since the eyes can only see a fraction of the world around a viewer, and vision is hampered in darkness, while the ability to localize a sound source works in all directions, to varying accuracy, regardless of the surrounding light.

Humans estimate the location of a source by taking cues derived from one ear (monaural cues), and by comparing cues received at both ears (difference cues or binaural cues). Among the difference cues are time differences of arrival and intensity differences. The monaural cues come from the interaction between the sound source and the human anatomy, in which the original source sound is modified before it enters the ear canal for processing by the auditory system.

The HRTF can also be described as the modifications to a sound from a direction in free air to the sound as it arrives at the eardrum. These modifications include the shape of the listener's outer ear, the shape of the listener's head and body, the acoustical characteristics of the space in which the sound is played, and so on. All these characteristics will influence how (or whether) a listener can accurately tell what direction a sound is coming from.

The HRTF can be synthesized electronically - using digital signal processing - and used to process various sound sources which can be delivered to a listener's ears via headphones (or loudspeakers). This creates a virtual sound image in three dimensions and can provide a stunning, immersive listening experience.

Hearing in three dimensions - When we listen to the sounds around us in the real world, we can determine with great accuracy where each individual sound source is. Our head and ears operate as a very sophisticated 'directional acoustic antenna system;' such that we are not only of the location and distance of the sound sources themselves but, also, of the type of acoustic environment which surrounds us.

Synthesizing 3D Audio - There are two main aspects to loudspeaker delivery of 3D audio. It is essential to ensure that the listener perceives the sounds via only a single HRTF and, secondly, that the trans-aural crosstalk is neutralized effectively.

During loudspeaker playback, trans-aural crosstalk occurs. This means that the left ear hears a little of what the right ear is hearing—after a small, additional time delay of around 0.25 ms—and vice versa. In order to prevent this from happening, appropriate 'crosstalk cancellation' signals must be created from the opposite loudspeaker.

Listening to 3D audio, via headphones, is not a recent phenomenon; it dates back to the 1930's when engineers at Bell Laboratories demonstrated an early form of an artificial head microphone system. Clearly, little or no trans-aural crosstalk occurs during headphone listening and so there is no need for crosstalk cancellation.

The Mozart Effect

The Mozart Effect is an inclusive term signifying the transformational powers of music in health, education, and well-being. It represents the use of music (and the arts) to

improve the health of families and communities.
improve memory, awareness, and the integration of learning styles.
improve listening and attention deficit disorders.
correct mental and physical disorders and injuries.
activate creativity and reduce depression and anxiety.

The Mozart Effect is an inclusive term signifying the transformational powers of music in health, education, and well-being. It represents the general use of music to reduce stress, depression, or anxiety; induce relaxation or sleep; activate the body; and improve memory or awareness. Innovative and experimental uses of music and sound can improve listening disorders, dyslexia, attention deficit disorder, autism, and other mental and physical disorders and injuries.

Research with Mozart's music began in France in the late 1950's when Dr. Alfred Tomatis began his experiments in auditory stimulation for children with speech and communication disorders. By 1990, there were hundreds of centers throughout the world using Mozart's music containing high frequencies, especially the violin concertos and symphonies, to help children with dyslexia, speech disorders, and autism.

In the 1990's experiments were begun at the University of California in Irvine with Mozart's music and spatial intelligence assessments. As recently as 2001, new studies in England were using Mozart's music to study its effect on epilepsy.

Mozart wrote more than six hundred major compositions during his lifetime, beginning at age five. The clarity, form, excellence of the performance, and frequency responses have all gone into the selection of this special series of Mozart's music. The music has been sequenced for different activities.

Music containing high frequency for stimulating the auditory system in the brain has been selected based on the work of Dr. Tomatis. Most current relaxation DVDs and tapes are slower and do not include the higher frequencies. The selections have been sequenced according to key, tempo, and a variety of other psychological, physiological, and aesthetic factors to achieve a variety of auditory, physical, and emotional responses.

Mozart's music is the most popular and researched music for helping modify attentiveness and alertness. The structure and, not overly emotional, expression helps clarify time/space perception. It is not over stimulating and the structures of the rondo, sonata-allegro form, and variation form are basic ways in which the brain becomes familiar with the development and familiarity of ideas.

Each learning environment should be assessed before using music. The time of day and the sounds in the environment such as air conditioners and outside sounds, all modify the way we concentrate. Each person responds to sound differently when tired or after having a meal. At times, ten minutes of stimulating music that quickens the heartbeat and awakens the imagination is useful (Marches, folk, popular). Dr. Georgi Lozanov suggests slow Baroque music for optimal learning (Bach, Handel, Correli, Telemann).

Some people are hyper-responsive to sound, and music can distract them during study. Others learn how to select music for their different moods and projects. Generally, the challenge to study comes when we are over stimulated and cannot settle down to focus, or we are dull, tired, or bored and cannot get the energy to begin a task.

Sound is the vibration field that makes up language, music, and tone. When it is organized, we communicate words, ideas, feelings, and expressions. In its disorganized form, it creates noise. Sound, whether we are in the womb or even in a coma, reaches our brain and our bodies through skin, bones, and ears. Every person listens in different ways. When rhythm, melody, and harmony are organized into beautiful forms, the mind, body, spirit, and emotions are brought toward harmony. There are dozens of ways in which sound and music is used throughout the world.

Music helps release the stresses of being ill: it can vitalize, inspire, and reduce pain. Music is not an instant cure for disease, although there is much research on the importance of auditory stimulation in health. The ear is essential for balance, language, expression, and spatial orientation. Music and rhythmic patterning are used extensively before and after surgery and for patients who have had strokes and head injuries.

Therapists, using music, are trained specialists who can assist in physical, developmental, and psychological settings. A musical background is not necessary for the patient. Music reaches multiple areas of the brain—more than just language—and, therefore, can be quite effective in a clinical environment.

There have been many different studies and, probably, a hundred different ways to measure intelligence. We know certain music brings us to greater attentiveness, allowing for better focus and concentration. Studies show that playing music early in life helps build the neural pathways that allow language, memory, and spatial development to take place.

We know that stimulating linguistic rhymes, dances, movement, and play, in the early years, are essential to the foundation of bringing the emotions, mind, and body together. Music can be effective in study and assist in concentration. A popular study, published in Nature Magazine in 1993, showed when students who listened to Mozart, prior to testing, they scored higher marks in an intelligence test.

The Middle Pillar Exercise

This is an exercise in sound, using synesthesia. As a form of chanting, it can be seen as a fundamental "re-tuning fork" for the human body. Synesthesia is the cross-modal translation of various senses where sound is experienced in consciousness as light or patterns of color. This phenomenon is very common in children under four and is, usually, no longer present after the child turns seven.

Over the centuries, the practice of Magick has been reserved for the ultra elite of Europe. Often considered a higher form of Physics, Magick is the art of changing consciousness at will. The Middle Pillar Exercise comes from centuries of that tradition and, more recently, from Golden Dawn chanting rituals.

The purpose of this ancient tradition is to create an exercise in visualization to allow this visualization to become an important tool of communication with the subconscious. The Middle Pillar Exercise is meant to influence the process of self-transformation.

Reproduced scientific evidence (Marks, 1975), now, indicates that there is a mutual-reinforcement between certain specific vibrated vowel-sounds and visualization experiences. This constitutes a visual-auditory synesthesia, or feedback system, where vowels evoke powerful visual "sensations."

The Middle Pillar Exercise corresponds with several forms of self-induced synesthesia or sensory blending. A reason is shown for retraining our eyes and ears out of habitual modes of sensory screening.

With this tool, we might free ourselves from certain conceptual restraints (belief systems) and upgrade our practice in the use of creative visualizations. This technique heals our culturally pre-programmed Cartesian duality (and the so-called mind-body split).

Synesthesia - Cross-Modal Translations of Sensory-Motor Inputs

Synesthesia is defined as sensory blending or melding; and any combination of the five senses may be involved simultaneously. The most common combinations are between visual-images and sound (colored-hearing) and visual-images produced by taste.

In perfumes, for example, the sense of smell evokes memory and its attendant images. There is a common core of similarities in synesthetic experiences. Visual colors are associated with speech sounds. There is evidence that everyone is capable of experiencing synesthesia.

Synesthesia may occur spontaneously or as a learned response. Middle Pillar Exercise (from classical Magick systems), with its simultaneous 'vibration of God-names' and visualizations, may be viewed as an 'access code.' This 'access code' is a helpful tool which opens creative relationships with different parts of the subconscious and the physical body (parasympathetic system).

When we are "caught up" in the meditative process, we experience cognitive meaning in sensory form. Psi information (as described in the previous book in this series, *ESP Induction through Forms of Self-Hypnosis*) is mediated via mental imagery. The image, and its "meaning," is identical. Therefore, psi communications are enhanced under conditions which facilitate imagery. Both Magical visualizations and creative imagination promote this viewpoint.

According to Archetypal Psychology, synesthesia is how imagination imagines. What this experience does is transform the singleness of any one sense out of its literalness. It makes a metaphor of sense perception, itself, as in the example, "I can see the music, and how it moves."

One of synesthesia's special roles is to summarize important cognitive distinctions in a convenient and economical way. As a shorthand, it is compact, but relatively fixed and, therefore, limited. Its validity as a useful tool appears to be limited to the context of magical practice.

Without a system for creating a meaningful experience, such as Pathworking, there is very little spiritual value in the phenomenon except the aesthetic. Researchers have considered synesthesia less significant in adulthood than childhood. This need not be true with the proper application, such as when using The Middle Pillar Exercise.

Traditional Technique

Proper control of the breath has been emphasized in, both, western and eastern meditation techniques. This, of course, connects with the sense of smell and posits us in the realm of Psyche (the breath-soul of the head whose passages are the nostrils).

Psyche's realm is "the place between"—the realm of soul-making. It is that place between the physical body and the abstractions of the spirit. Note the semantic similarity between 'psi' and 'Psyche.' In The Qabalah (QBL) this internal space is called Tiphareth, the realm of imagination.

The Middle Pillar Exercise is designed so that the actual formation of the body/mind system may be changed and renewed. It is not concerned with the exclusive cultivation of, either, the body or consciousness.

> *"Always in a salutary way is the path between the two extremes indicated."*
>
> FRANCIS ISRAEL REGARDIE

The vibration of god-names, as well as stimulating the vision in specific directions, stimulates the endocrine system and glands in the mid-brain by a resonance effect. These effects are not necessarily to be viewed as causal (the result of previous action), but are perceived simultaneously; their reciprocal relationship is inherent.

This is another way to see how information (like sound) can be a resolution of the hologram, where detail and content are further layers within the other.

New Model

We may presume to use current scientific research to upgrade our practice of The Middle Pillar Exercise. Through the inherent mutual reinforcement phenomena of visual-auditory systems, when we Middle Pillar, we induce synesthesia at will.

The next obvious question is: *"Why would we want to induce synesthesia?"* When we are experiencing the creative imagination, that engagement with an image, all modes of perception meld into indivisible unity. This form of systematic cross modal matching is closely allied with the concept of a system of correspondences.

Significance is not found in analysis, but in the image itself. The image consists of such apparently diverse elements as behavior, fantasy, thoughts, dreams, illness, etc. None of these are 'because of' the image'; they are the image itself as a 'just-so' story. To form a "ground" for our spirituality in the imaginal realm (internal topography), we must re-imagine the Creation.

Re-imagining the Creation is, precisely, the function of The Middle Pillar Exercise. It is a dramatization of the *Creation Myth*.

> *The creation of the world becomes the archetype of every human gesture, whatever its plane of reference may be…communication with heaven is expressed by variants of the cosmic pillar, which stands at the center of the world.*
>
> MIRCEA ELIADE —THE SACRED AND THE PROFANE

This pillar is a useful symbol for, what we shall term, the ego-Self axis. This axis is a relationship built up through various psychological exercises. It forms the link between ego-consciousness and our Higher Self.

The Higher Self represents, both, conscious and subconscious minds working together in harmony. In psychology, this is termed the Transcendent Function. It establishes our relationship to the cosmos, namely, a conscious relationship to outer/inner space. As in synesthesia, we are returned to the magical, child-like mode where cognitive meaning is in sensory form. In this experience, careful aesthetic elaboration of a psychic event is its meaning.

One can learn to experience this mode of consciousness in a ritual situation. Once (re-)learned, it can extend into every sensory experience of daily life, either literal or metaphorical.

The sense of inherent meaningful importance in day-to-day events, and trivia, is a necessary concern of the soul. Through it, 'life makes sense' and 'sense makes life'. The alchemists always stressed identity of the physical/spiritual connection.

The roots for the word 'sense' mean something which is directly tangible — physical and solid or concrete. It also, now, implies something meaningful and significant. Imagination takes place wherever we are. When you split sensory data from meaning, we not only split sensation from intuition, you also split spirit, soul, and body.

The conjunction of concrete sensation, psychic image, and spiritual meaning is aesthesis which denotes breathing in (smelling) and perceiving. In ritual, all the senses are directly involved via the correspondence system. This creates a mood, or atmosphere, which the participant "breathes in." There is an experience of unity of the senses via synesthetic metaphor.

Techniques:

The guidelines for inducing visual-auditory synesthesia are straight forward:

1. Vowels are an especially powerful source for production of secondary visual sensations.

2. There is a correlation between auditory pitch and visual brightness. The brightness of vowels varies and photisms, visual images of light, vary in brightness as the sounds that produce them varies in their frequency.

3. Visual pitch predicts the whiteness or blackness of associated photisms.

4. Visual size increases as auditory pitch decreases: the louder the vowel-sound, the larger the image. However, induced size is not related solely to pitch.

Vowel-Sounds and Color Correspondences				
Pronunciation	**Vowel**	**Color**	**Properties**	**Frequency**
"mama"	a	red & yellow	bright	
"late", "let"	e	white	brightest	high pitch
"bit", "beet"	i	white	brightest	low pitch
"home"	o	red & black	"grave'	dark pitch
"boot"	u	dark colors	deep blue	darkest pitch
	ou	black		dark

Order of increasing frequency (pitches): u, o, a, e, i.

Order if increasing vowel brightness: u, ou, o, a, e, i.

Example: The God-name, IAO, begins with a bright vowel and concludes with a dark vowel. The center vowel may be considered the melding point or median.

The above information indicates that we might be able to learn to pitch the magical voice, and loudness, to induce a desired visual effect. This eliminates any sense of detachment from our experience or activity. This is an experience of the immortal body or philosopher's stone.

4

SOCIAL SEXUAL

EARTH TRIGRAM

HISTORIC CONTEXT— *The sciences were changing in the 1960s, with the emergence of Social Anthropology and the concept that beliefs might be something more than just about faith. To be able to change a belief system at will (choice alone) was considered paranormal, and could lead to a super soldier.*

James Hillman was just emerging with his work in Imaginal Psychology, now considered part of the Archetypal Psychology (3rd Generation Carl Jung) movement. The concept of an archetype allowed doors of perception to open, thereby allowing more access to the physical world.

The historic context is when his work connected the psyche with the Soul; it allowed access to higher states of consciousness. This was seen as a whole new realm for exploration, and possible lead to being closer to relationship (indigenous-like) to the Earth.

Chapter Four

Belief Systems & Change of Values

Huzur Maharaj Ji was once asked in London in the 70's, "How do you do it?" "Do what?" was Master's reply. "How do you manage to look so good?" The answer sums up the actions and character of a perfect disciple and, of course, a perfect Master. "I look good because I don't do anything I shouldn't do."

—HUZUR MAHARAJ JI

James Hillman's latest book title (Jungian Imaginal Psychology) is titled *"The Soul's Code: In Search of Character and Calling."* Each of us has developed a series of "callings," those parts of Self we seek to fulfill throughout our life. Most of us, however, tend to fall into more circular forms of behavior where these goals and directions are never actually achieved.

These specific "calls" are, mostly, focused around our belief systems. These calls were, probably, formed in earlier parts of our life where they are they no longer applicable, or even functional, toward meeting our current goals and needs in life. Our challenge is, to somehow, find a way to break these limitations, world-views, or beliefs on what we might actually achieve during our life.

Steve Gaskin's *"Monday Night Class"* was first to refer to the importance of how these first layers of beliefs were imprinted according to how we were born. Later called *"Spiritual Midwifery,"* most of our current belief systems are first formed or originate from pre-natal and post-natal traumas. Circumcision, for example, can set up beliefs about that part of the body that will follow one all through his life in such lifestyles as sports.

More often than not, however, those beliefs are no longer valid or even functional for current situations and lifestyle directions. To get a better realization of this concept, imagine how a dog is whelped in a litter. The physical world experience, for the dog, is being surrounded by love. This is the reason the dog can offer more serious states of love and devotion to our well-being.

Belief Systems

Belief is usually defined as a conviction to the truth of a proposition. Beliefs can be acquired through perception, contemplation or communication. In a psychological view, belief is a representational mental state that takes the form of a propositional attitude.

> *In the religious sense, "belief" refers to a part of a wider spiritual or moral foundation, generally called faith; historically generated by a group's need to provide a functionally valid foundation to sustain them. The generally accepted faiths usually note that when oppressive states are generated by it being exercised, and not a fact of reality, it was in need of more revelation or clarification.* [WIKIPEDIA]

> *(be and lyian, to hold dear) – That state of the mind by which it assents to propositions, not by reason of their intrinsic evidence, but because of authority.* [CATHOLIC ENCYCLOPEDIA]

The word faith has various meanings. The central meaning is similar to "belief", "trust" or "confidence" but, unlike these words, "faith" tends to imply a transpersonal, rather than interpersonal, relationship – with God or a higher power. The object of faith can be a person, an inanimate object, or state of affairs. It might, also, be a proposition or body of propositions, such as a religious credo.

In each case, however, faith is in an aspect of the object and cannot be logically proven or objectively known. Faith can, also, be defined as accepting something as true because we have been told it is true by someone who we believe and trust. In its truest form, faith means trusting the word of another.

Belief is considered propositional in that it is an assertion, claim or expectation about reality that is presumed to be either true or false. This applies even if this cannot be practically determined, such as a belief in the existence of a particular deity. It is these "assumed truths" that, ultimately, limit what we can become and complete during our lifetime.

In the movie, *What the Bleep*, reference was made to Indians being unable to see ships on the horizon because they had no concepts of such a possibility. The big question is, would a staunch Christian (personal belief) be able to see two liens if they walked in the door? Our beliefs shape our reality, including these possibilities

> *"I would not have seen it if I had not believed it."*
>
> OLD SELMA CARTEL SAYING

Historically, philosophical attempts to analyze the nature of belief have been couched in terms of judgment. David Hume and Immanuel Kant are both, particularly, well known for their analyses using this framework. Distinctions are made between the formation of "natural law" and that called "civil law."

There is a difference between belief and being. Those who are unaware of being aware are believers. Those who are aware are not believers, as being aware has no use for belief. If we are going to believe in something, that would suggest, only, that we possess reservations about that which we aim to believe.

If we are aware, embodied in flesh, and living in the present, then there is nothing to believe in. There is a fine line between belief and unbelief, just as there is between matter and spirit and all the dualities.

Everything is in the metaphor. The perception of darkness differs from the mere absence of light due to the effects of after images on perception. In perceiving, the eye is active, and that part of the retina that is unstimulated, produces a complementary afterimage.

The Purpose of Doubt

We, generally, know when we wish to ask a question and when we wish to pronounce a judgment. There is dissimilarity between the sensation of doubting and that of believing, but this is not all which distinguishes doubt from belief. There is, also, a practical difference. Our beliefs guide our desires and shape our actions.

Doubt is an uneasy and dissatisfied state from which we struggle to free ourselves. What we want is to pass into the state of belief; where belief in the latter is a calm and satisfactory state which we do not wish to avoid or to change to a belief in anything else. On the contrary, we cling, tenaciously, not merely to believing, but to believing just what we do believe.

Thus, both, doubt and belief have positive effects upon us, though very different ones. Belief does not make us act at once, but puts us into such a condition that we shall behave in a certain way when the occasion arises.

Doubt has not the least such active effect, but stimulates us to inquiry until it is destroyed. This reminds us of the irritation of a nerve and the reflex action produced thereby; while for the analogue of belief, in the nervous system, we must look to what are called nervous associations such as the habit of nerves which makes the mouth water upon smelling a peach.

The irritation of doubt causes a struggle to attain a state of belief. I shall term this struggle inquiry, though it must be admitted that this is, sometimes, not a very apt designation. The irritation of doubt is the only immediate motive for the struggle to attain belief. Belief is of the nature of a habit.

The "voice of reason" and the "voice of coyote" speak as different points of view. The voice of reason is "inside the box" and is very comfortable (safe). The other, often associated with risk, is stepping "outside the box," taking a chance for a better result. This is the moment we can sense our own limitations.

It turns out that the "voice of reason" and the "voice of coyote" are, in fact, the same voice, but at different levels of our relationship to the higher Self. The peaceful, and sympathetic, will find it hard to resist the temptation to submit opinions to authority. Most of all, we must admire the method of tenacity for its strength, simplicity, and directness. Persistence and tenacity, alone, will win the day, even over unrewarded genius.

Men who pursue persistence and tenacity are distinguished for their decision of character which becomes very easy with such a mental rule. They do not waste time in trying to make up their minds on what they want. Upon whatever alternative comes first, they hold to it to the end no matter what happens, without an instant of irresolution.

This is one of the splendid qualities which, generally, accompany brilliant, long-lasting success. It is impossible not to envy the person who can dismiss reason, although we know how it must turn out in the end.

Internal Maps of Reality

Certain unconscious aspects of Self will fight our desire to make changes in our belief systems. This is what is called our internal map of reality. It includes beliefs, values, strategies, decisions, and basic ways we arbitrarily conduct our life. These ways of thinking, and behaving, were created while we were growing up, so we could feel safe in our family.

We, unconsciously, associate the old way with safety, so anything that starts to change it triggers resistance, even when we want the change on a conscious level. Habits, for example, take three full months of active participation before they become part of our internal and normal response.

Sensory inputs, as they come in, are filtered in several ways. It is these filtering systems that make up a significant part of our internal map of reality. Everyone's different, but these filters include our beliefs, values, memories, and decisions. The internal language used, retrieval protocols, our various strengths, and strategies for making decisions are, also, part of our filter systems.

The purpose of these filters is to accomplish three basic actions: delete, distort, and generalize. There is far too much data coming through your senses. The deletion process happens automatically, quickly, and totally unconsciously. We all tend to delete whatever does not agree with our current beliefs or values.

We, also, tend to distort what comes in so that it verifies what we already believe and value. From the movie "What the Bleep," the Indian could not see the ship at sea because his world-view did not include such concepts. It was not until the Shaman asked, "What is that out in the water?" that the Indians could, then, see something (the ship) floating in the water.

It is the third purpose of these filters which does not allow us to see the differences that make something unique. One clue that generalizations are being made is when we hear words like "all, never, always, no one, everyone" - global words. This is the purpose of filters, to delete, distort, and generalize input. They do this automatically, rapidly and almost always, unconsciously.

When making a complex matrix of internal representations, we, also, generate two main responses. The first response deals with feelings and kinesthetic sensations or the physical and emotional states that associated with the memory (or experience). This might include being happy or sad, depressed or elated, being motivated, or a myriad of other rich and complex emotions.

The second response is our behaviors. Feelings, behaviors, and these internal representations are like a circular loop. Feelings and physical states help generate behaviors (and internal representations), while behaviors help generate feelings (and those internal representations). In turn, internal representations generate, both, feelings and behaviors.

As an example, we can change our state, or mood, by changing posture such as how we hold and move your body and, also, by changing our breathing. To create what you want in life will require going out into the world and looking for the parts of this system that we can influence and change to create the states, behaviors, and outcomes we seek.

These filtering mechanisms pretty much happen unconsciously and automatically. Our ways of filtering with our beliefs and values, ultimately, create all the nuances of our life, and how we experience it. It is our beliefs and values which create the current movie we enjoy.

If we can take charge of these things, and choose how we do them instead of having them just run on automatic, we can make huge changes in how we experienced life. More importantly, we can determine what kinds of outcomes are available with those filters.

Rules of Belief Systems

There are a number of important principles associated with beliefs.

1. From our early life interactions and experiences (from our primary caregivers), we all develop beliefs about who we are and what our relationship is to the rest of the world. We do not really get to choose these beliefs as they form when we are too small to evaluate them. They become core-components of how we see ourselves, other people, and the world.

2. Our beliefs (along with other aspects of our internal map of reality) create the results, circumstances, and basic experiences of our life. Regardless of what we believe, we will find a way to create consistency between our life and beliefs. For this reason, beliefs, for the believer, are always true.

The brain is a goal-seeking mechanism and a very powerful one. Our brain will, either, make whatever we believe in to come true in our life. Or it will, at least, make it appear to be true which amounts to the same thing, as far as our life experiences are concerned.

We can arrange to be right about our beliefs, just by creating the circumstances that confirm what the truth of what we believe is true. This works in one (or more) of the following three ways:

We will attract, and be attracted to, people and situations that confirm the truth of what we believe. If we believe that no one will ever love us, we will "somehow" feel a magical attraction to those who do not have the capacity to love.

Whatever we believe, we will exhibit a magnetic attraction for people and situations that will help us be right about our belief.

We will find ways to distort what we perceive so as to make a belief seem true. Believing that no one will ever love us, we, then, interpret other people's behavior as evidence that they don't love us.

If we believe we will never be prosperous, we will find a way to interpret whatever situation we are in as lacking prosperity. Of all the possible interpretations in any situation, we will pick those that confirm that our belief is true and will, then, filter out any other interpretations that contradict our belief.

We will act in such a way that people will, finally, comply with what we believe and act in a way that confirms our belief to be true. The fear of not being loved will make that a self-serving prophecy. If we believe we will be poor, we will, finally, act in such a way that circumstances prove our belief to be right.

3: Significant negative emotional experiences create beliefs that are not resourceful and cause us to focus on what we do not want. Since the mind takes whatever we focus on as an instruction to create something, this is not resourceful. It does not serve you. To get what we want, we have to focus on what we want and have beliefs that tell the mind to create that result.

When we notice our self focusing on what we do not want, we must immediately change our focus to what we do want. Our mind doesn't know when we focus on something that we do not want it. It always takes whatever we focus on as an instruction to go get something and bring it to us or make something happen.

For this reason, it is crucial that we, immediately, replace thoughts of what we do not want (beliefs that create negative outcomes) with thoughts of what we do want.

4: Since everything is true to the person who believes it, evaluating beliefs based on whether they are "true" or "false" is not useful. Doing so is indulging in circular, fallacious logic. Conscious, happy people evaluate beliefs based on whether of not they are resourceful—on whether or not they create the desired results and experience of life.

Beliefs have consequences, and the best way to evaluate a belief is by what consequences it creates. Since all beliefs are true to the believer, believing something "because it is true" is useless and, often, dangerous.

5: The most effective way to replace beliefs that do not serve us is to adopt the "witness" posture which means to watch the process of how a belief creates the results of our life. This "witnessing" process causes whatever is not resourceful to fall away and whatever is resourceful to remain.

If we think something outside of us is creating your experience or outcome, we will be unable to witness what is happening. Instead, our awareness will be busy looking for something to blame. This phenomenon is called "projection of the shadow."

6: Once we have watched the creative process (with awareness), this will cause non-resourceful beliefs to fall away. We, then, consciously choose a more resourceful belief that creates the mental, emotional, spiritual, and physical results sought.

Beliefs are nothing more than instructions to our mind to make something happen in our life. We should not accept results we do not seek which are created by beliefs we did not choose. We can, then, consciously choose more resourceful beliefs and, in doing so, now, create whatever results we seek.

7: Discovering our core beliefs is the first step in the process of replacing automatic, unconscious, and un-resourceful beliefs with more conscious and resourceful beliefs. To begin this process, make a list of ways we could complete the following sentences:

"I am _____."

"People are _____."

"The world is _____."

Examples would include: *"The world is filled with abundance"*; *"People are basically good"*; *"Everything happens for a reason"*; *"everything leads to something better."* If we really believed these things, we will create them in our life. That is how simply it all works.

8: The most effective way to determine our core beliefs is to examine the results we are getting. Are they allowing us to achieve our goals? If not, it may be time to take a closer look at why.

9: As long as we continue to hold the same beliefs, we will continue to get the same results. There is no way to continue to hold the same beliefs and get different results. To get different results, we must be willing to adopt different beliefs. First, we must decide what results we want and, then, determine what beliefs would create these results. Then, adopt those beliefs. When we do, we will get the results implied in those beliefs.

10: To install a new belief, we must focus on it as often as possible and in every way we can – like leaving notes at important change nodes (like a refrigerator, to lose weight).

Meditation, especially with brain remapping technologies, greatly speeds up this process. It helps us become more consciously aware of what we are creating and it takes the emotional charge out of things in our life. This allows us to look at our life, and what happens within it, from a more dispassionate perspective. In other words, to be the witness instead of the player.

How to Change Values

To begin this process, we must first know what the values are. This is called forming the "hierarchy of values." There is a process that helps facilitate this list. We begin by asking our self, "What is my most important value?" Then, continue on with what is the second and third set of values? Do this list until the are between ten or twelve values on the list.

A basic list, usually, includes the following key words as seen in the list below. New words may become added as we continue this process. Some of the words may change or become more to each of us. Some of us may relate more with love to physical contact while others feel more toward learning with inspiration.

Truth
Honesty/Integrity
Freedom
Security
Love/Physical Contact
Adventure
Peace/Harmony/Getting Along
Excitement
Beauty/Nature
Consistency
Learning/Growing
Connection/Friendship/Community/Family
Balance
Completion/Follow-Through
Efficiency
Spiritual Awareness
Creativity

Creating a Hierarchy of Values

After the list is created, we must look for conflicts in this list and those values that do not serve us. Take the time, now, to arrange this list in order of important, allowing it to show us our most important value first and least important value last. Another process, which questions our first response, will change this list. Everyone's list will be different and there is no right or wrong here. By attempting to define these values, we have created a "container" from which we can use them (as tools).

We, often, have different values in different areas of our life such as our values toward our career, relationships, parenting, and the spiritual realm. Start with the broader category of life values. Once we have these in hand, we will, then, want to "chunk down" this process into other areas of our life. This is when changing our belief becomes a real tool and not just a driver.

For me, Magick has always been the primary focus in my life, representing a higher form of Physics. Using that as my life guide, all of my rituals have been oriented around spiritual awareness and not material gain. No matter what that cost, it was worth the personal growth involved.

It, also, led me toward the goals I sought – toward the personal evolution of my own consciousness. While friendships represent the highest form of love (Thelema), I make a distinction between friendship and spirituality. In my belief system, I place spirituality over love. This is a personal choice, however, and can vary within each of us.

When doing this process, it is, often, easier to have a close friend ask the questions rather than doing both the questions and responses our self. Self-honesty is critical. There is no point in creating a list of what we think our values should be. We must ask our self, *"What is important about life?"*, then, write down the exact words that come to us.

When we get to a point where the obvious surface values emerge, we must decide if there are some others that we did not yet think of at first. Often, the more important values come out later. Now, we need o remember a time when we were really motivated and try to identify the feeling we had just before we felt that motivation.

It is most likely a value. Doing this, repeatedly, will lead to realizing that we are getting the same feelings again. What is motivating us are the primary values that direct our life. Once this list has become better developed, we must ask our self (or use a partner): "*Is A more important than B or is B more important than A?*"

If when making a comparison you hit a roadblock and the answer is not obvious we would like, we can ask our self, "*If I could have value A, but not B, would that work? Which is more important?*" This may create some internal struggle and further insight about our self and our values. Once we have compared this top value to all others, we will know it is our most important value.

Sometimes, another value may turn out to be more important than the one we first thought was number one" on our list. Even though this process may seem a bit tedious, continue to compare each value to all the others. Quite often, our first impulse is not accurate. Everyone should be required to do this process as it helps in identifying what is and is not as important.

Determining Conflicts in Values

Once the "hierarchy of values" list has been established, determine if any of these values are in conflict with any others. "*Can I have A and B at the same time or do they conflict with each other?*" After asking these questions, we must, carefully, note what comes to us and write these thoughts down in our own words. Some will be descriptions of what we seek; other will be what we do not seek.

Using the value of honesty, for example, ask "*Why is honesty important?*" Our response might be "*Because if I am not honest, I will get into trouble.*" Conversely, we might, also, have said, "*Because I don' t want to consequences of being dishonest.*" Or, "*I feel good when I know I' m honest.*"

The first two are descriptions of what we don't want (trouble, or bad consequences). The third answer describes something we are moving toward, feeling good about our self. This value, also, tells us if we are moving away from dishonesty just to avoid it or we are moving toward honesty which would be the better choice.

We have to check inside our self, and then decide to what degree we are motivated with this value. We must make the determination on how much we do not want to how much we do want. It is important to be honest with our self so these values can take their proper position in the scheme of our hierarchy of values. Being honest can be shaped by our beliefs and desires.

The reason moving away from what we do not want is NOT resourceful is because to move away from something makes internal pictures (and dialog) with what we do not want. To move away from something requires our mind to focus on it.

Here is where it gets tricky. We cannot tell our mind what we do not want when it is busy creating what we are focusing on. So, if we are focusing on what we do not want, our mind works on that and we, often, end up getting exactly what we did not want. The thought, itself, will (most likely) make it happen as stated in the following quote:

> *"Anything not specifically forbidden is mandatory."*
>
> - MERLIN

It is, now, time to look at each value and determine how much time we spend fulfilling each one. We should confirm to our self that the top values on our list are where we spend most of our effort. We must, then, decide if the results we are getting from having these values be the most important is really what we are seeking.

I we are having health problems, for example, but health does not appear on your list of values or it is way down the list, this may be a clue to why we are creating poor health. If health is important to us, we must ask our self why we are not spending more time on creating it for our self. We might, then, want to

114

reconsider its importance of health in our scheme of things and move it to a more appropriate location in our hierarchy of values.

Many Jungian Psycho-therapy models suggest that all illnesses are ways the subconscious tries to communicate and get the attention of the conscious mind. Once the consciousness "gets it" (understands the importance of the message), there is no further need of the illness. This is the nature of our thoughts and beliefs.

Our values create, and limit, what you your universe might offer. By rearranging them in order of importance in our life, they become tools rather than drivers. This does not mean that we can, necessarily, simply discard the values that appear less important. Some values are like old clothing, very familiar and comfortable to wear. We must learn to determine which values may not allow us to achieve our immediate goal or mission and which ones hinder or limit our success. We can, then, tuck them away for a possible re-examination later.

As a metaphor, I have a pair of bell-bottom pants I will never again fit in (32-inch waist). They are neatly folded in a bottom drawer, stored for a time when…. This is the drawer that holds many of my most important values and feelings in life.

To Summarize

1. Elicit our values by asking "*What is important about life?*"

2. Arrange these values in the order of importance.

3. Look for values that conflict with each other.

4. Look for values that actually represent something we want to avoid or move away from.

5. Check to see if we really are spending the most time and energy with our most top values on our list.

6. Check to see what is missing, and why we are not motivated to do anything about them?

7. Check to see if any of the values on your list are creating problems.

An example of number seven might be money, especially if it were number one on our hierarchy of values. Pursuing and having it may not lead to happiness or making us a pleasant person to be around. Making other people happy might not be healthy if it is too high on the list and not allowing us to pursue what we want to do with our life.

During this process, the unconscious part of our self may fight our consciousness. Just watch it happen and keep going. After we "witness" our behavior, and how it is not being effective with our goals and plans, we can, then, take a closer inspection of our values, and begin (methodically) changing them, just like we would change our clothing.

A Brain Remapping Exercise

Death is the end of life in a biological organism, marked by the full cessation of its vital functions. All known multicellular living things eventually die, whether because of natural causes such as disease, or unnatural ones such as accidents. Death has, also, been personified, throughout history, as a figure to be feared and hated.

Imagine a world without a fear of death? Considering the fact that fear, and avoidance, dictate most of our attitudes toward death, it is a challenge to imagine a completely different scenario. There are many ways to confront our own mortality. However, those people facing a terminal illness know that the "when" factor changes everything.

Knowledge of our probable exit date can blast holes in all but the most solid walls of denial. The following link is a website offering a way to calculate your approximate time of death based on age, weight and height, and several other variables: http://www.deathclock.com/

In our future, we will impart the sacred gift of predestined death timing to young adults, at puberty, in a rite of passage. As the adolescent initiates become capable of creating life, they are required to receive and contemplate the awe-inspiring foreknowledge of their appointed date with death.

It would change our culture in that, then, the "terrorism MEM" could no longer exist. Everyone's moment would be held sacred, much like when making love (sacred time, timelessness). We would be less nihilistic in our world-view and would have no reason to abuse another, being more "in the moment."

Twenty years ago, I encountered Kaplan-Williams' Journal book on the Senoi people of Malaysia. Senoi families would sit around the breakfast table each morning, talking about their dreams. For the Senoi (and Hopi), dreams formed the centerpiece of their life, guiding every aspect of existence.

Children, in their earliest ages, are taught how to transform dream monsters into allies. More importantly, they learn how to increase their capacity for pleasure.

"Pleasure is a safer guide than either right or duty." - SAMUEL BUTLER

This was done by pursuing their dreams passionately and creatively. Exploring dreams can help us find our special talents. In addition, everyone in the Senoi culture learns how to identify big dreams which hold information that must be shared with the entire community.

Since all Senoi have been informed of their predestined death timing (when they are going to die), everyone celebrates their own "Death Day" each year. This is done as we would celebrate our birthdays. Children grow up knowing how long their parents will accompany them in physical form and they know who will care for them if both parents die before they grow up.

Even the smallest children are included in conversations about the facts of death just as they are included in discussions about the facts of life. Parents use words the children understand and no one uses euphemisms when talking about death. Every question and concern is addressed with honesty and respect.

With the Senoi, in addition to practical and esoteric instruction in matters relating to death, there is, also, a lot of joking about it. Black humor permeates every form of media and it shows up in all but the most sacred death rituals. Even memorial services, which are actually big celebrations called "awakes," are not immune to practical jokes and displays of debauchery.

There is, always, at least one trickster in every family. During the occasional "awake," a person might be found naked, their face painted black, walking across the middle of the food table. This jokester is regarded as the holiest of holies because she makes fun even in the face of death. Little children, often, dance behind the jokester, learning by example that there is nothing to fear.

In dreams, there is an appreciation for time as-an-ocean, where all things of the past, present and future exist simultaneously. Information, from any time/space, is readily available to anyone who is facile in traversing time through dreams or shamanic journeying or for those skilled with altered states of consciousness.

Time is not seen as a linear function, except where such convention helps people meet at a particular moment not discernible by sun or moon activity. Also, since everyone knows the future already exists, the Senoi speak of it with as much ease or comfort as they talk about the past.

No one harbors any delusions about manipulating or controlling the unfolding of life. With this orientation, the Senoi have little 'future-planning' or speculations about the future. While some sort of future does exist, it is not ever a very strong focus of their attention.

On the other hand, people retain their childlike curiosity and enthusiasm for life-to-come, in the same way we might get excited about an upcoming event we have been planning with friends. Even though we know in advance when and where something will happen, our experience of the event will be much different from our imagination of it.

> *Instead of making the "time of death a mystery," the Senoi focus on "the mystery of death" itself.*
>
> - SENOI DREAM MANUEL

They appreciate this difference, realizing that good planning can enhance an experience by anticipating one's needs, yet still providing enough structure to support personal expression and creative interaction. This respect for good planning, also, applies to death.

Foreknowledge of death timing is valued not only because it enhances the experience of dying, but, also, because it enhances the experience of living. Since people already know their death dates, they do not waste time obsessing about how to "prolong longevity" as we might. Instead of making the time of death a mystery, they can focus on the mystery of death itself.

Death by Appointment

In some cultures, spiritual masters maintain that the most enlightened attitude toward death is to act as if each moment is our last (like the Klingon "It's a good day to die" philosophy). But, if we really acted as if this is our last moment, would we buy groceries for tomorrow's dinner? Would we make plans for next weekend? Would we pay next month's rent or mortgage? Would we have children?

Such a tenet may stimulate a lot of good meditations and it, certainly, offers a valuable edge for living in the present. Predestined death can be overturned in an instant by a cosmic wild card. Although we might use this notion of "death-at-any-moment" to stay our toes, most of us will not, honestly, believe that that this is our last moment. And, our subsequent actions follow this belief.

In general, the human brain struggles mightily against the fact of its own mortality. The trick of acting as if we could die anytime is just that - a trick. What counts is how we feel, and how we act on what we feel. If we think we could die anytime, yet we are busy making plans and restocking writing supplies and buying bags full of groceries, it is questionable which belief is actually running us.

Maybe it is not enlightened to try and live enlightenment to act "as if" we could die anytime. Perhaps it is as silly as signing up for a four-year college program and, then, acting as if every class is our last. At some point, our schoolmates may begin to wonder if we are not a bit daft if we show up every day in our cap and gown ready to graduate at any moment.

We should not deny the fact that death can strike at any moment. We should be encouraged to remember our mortality, even if their only option is to deny it. There is another alternate path (an alternative is something already set in stone usually being a less probable choice in populations) that acknowledges death's ability to preempt my life while, also acknowledging that it has a date for each of us.

Here are many various URLs on Life Extension and Health which suggest that our pre-destined death dates ARE re-negotiable.

If there was less fear and mass hypnosis concerning death, foreknowledge of our death timing would bubble up, upon request, from the collective unconscious. It might come from dreams, body messages, or spiritual helpers or worldly omens.

For example, there are many stories about people intuiting their death timing as it draws near. A friend's grandfather, during a holiday dinner in the mid-1970s, announced that he didn't think he would be present for the following year's gathering. Everyone discounted his words, except my friend. She knew he knew, and wrote him a little note of acknowledgment, saying she believed and loved him. He died suddenly the following spring.

There are no many of us in modern culture who love and honor death as a friend, so we must use dreams to communicate about our relationship with death. This is not about creative visualization. In shamanism, if we experience something, it is real. It doesn't matter what level of reality is involved. At some level, it is all real.

What would it take for us to want to know about our death timing in advance? We would, first, need to come to peace with death, in general, before we could receive information about our own death. If we fear death, the foreknowledge of predestined death timing could wreak havoc in our lives.

Exposure to this information, without first providing years of spiritual preparation, would be as foolish as giving a knife to a two-year-old child. This is, also, one definition for the requirement of being a Saint as they know, and choose, their time of death.

There is much work ahead to changing our attitudes toward death. We are only now beginning to face death in ways that show respect for its beauty and its intrinsic value to life.

Predicting Death

Prognostication, as an art, refers to prediction and communication about future health. Prognostication relates not only to predicting death, but other outcome states such as what percentage of patients with a cancer of a certain stage on initial presentation will eventually develop meta-static disease.

Of three traditional domains of medicine (diagnosis, therapy, and prognosis), prognosis has received relatively little attention in modern medical training and research. It is easier to predict when death will occur for patients with some illnesses than for others. Proper prognosis, at the end, of life enables better decision making about care options and planning for patients and families.

We all desire and fear certainty. A desire for certainty arises in response to apparent chaos in the world. Fear arises because not all that is certain is good. Certainty, also, negates ambiguity and possibility, wherein we find hope that we can alter a problematic future. Therefore, an intense desire arises for some magic formula that will erase such uncertainty.

While we may lament our lack of control over "bad" outcomes such as death, the ability to predict and know the future represents a form of control if the future unfolds as predicted. Many studies have been devoted to a search for certainty in predicting death, often with little to show for it. It can be very disturbing to us that dying is a process, largely, beyond mortal control.

Prediction of death is not linear. It is like predicting the weather. We are good at predicting that rain will fall on a certain day, two to five days beforehand, but we cannot make such a prediction a month in advance. In the ultra-short range, it defies our abilities to predict exactly when the next raindrop will hit a finger.

Similarly, we are fairly good at predicting that a patient is at a high risk of dying over a matter of several months. For certain diseases, especially cancer, we are reasonably good at predicting death over a matter of weeks. It is usually impossible to predict the exact moment of death. Most approaches to predicting death use a grouping of diagnostic criteria and apply them at a certain point in time to establish a probability of dying at some time in the future.

The major problem with these approaches is that they are usually discrete, one-time predictions. Real clinical prognostication is more iterative, a form of "fuzzy logic." That is, the most valuable prognostic tool is to note the magnitude of change observed since the last prediction and incorporate this change into a new prediction.

122

For most serious and chronic disease processes, the earlier trend of an illness is the best predictor of the future trend. Patients whose clinical decline is rapidly accelerating will, likely, die sooner than those with identical clinical parameters who, for whatever reason, decline more slowly.

The Fantasy Death

Let us bring things closer to home. How do we want to die? The question is not whether we wish to die, but given that we have no choice in the matter, what would be our preference? Many of us are taken aback by these questions and have trouble answering them. Some of us answer immediately, as if we have been waiting for someone to ask us. There are a wide variety of responses. Nevertheless, there are some persistent themes. They suggest common hopes and fears about dying.

The first respondent might imagine dying suddenly in their asleep. An interesting variation on this theme concerned a newly married woman who hoped to die instantly, and unknowingly, with her husband, in a plane explosion on the way back from a vacation in the Caribbean.

These sudden-death fantasies highlight a fear, shared by many of us, that dying will be painful and difficult. The best we can hope for is simply to disappear. As Woody Allen put it, *"It's not that I'm afraid to die ... I just don't want to be there when it happens."* When such a sudden-death fantasy first expressed in a group setting, there is usually sympathetic, embarrassed laughter by those in the group.

We might hear someone mention that what might be seen as "winning the game" by the dying individual, may be viewed as the greatest of tragedies by family and friends. This was shown in the example of the fantasy with the newlywed who died to trump this concern by dying, spontaneously, with her husband. Couples in a common spousal game may even discuss who "wins" based on who dies first. Often, the first to die is seen as the winner as the bereaved is left to mourn.

The second-most-common fantasy death takes place at home. Typically, participants describe a peaceful scene. In advanced, but previously healthy old age, the dying person lies on the deathbed surrounded by family and friends. The home may be a literal home, a summer get-away cottage, or a fantasy home.

In this fantasy, people usually say they know they are dying. We, then, ask, *"How much warning would you like to have if you to be told you are dying?"* Responses vary, but two weeks is common. The challenge in this question is that respondents are struggling between a sense that there is something to accomplish in dying (at least goodbyes to be said) and the fact that dying is still a scary business.

Even in fantasy deaths, in which everybody is always physically comfortable, simply knowing they are to die soon is stressful. In fact, patients who get only two weeks notice usually perceive, and are perceived, as having, virtually, no time to come to grips with dying.

The third-most-common fantasy is dying while engaged in a valued or meaningful activity, often in a beautiful natural setting. A golfer wanted to die after a hole-in-one on the 18th hole. A mountain climber actually wanted to die with a rope breaking. A revolutionary wanted to die in a revolutionary struggle. Often, people describe pastoral scenes, dying on a mountaintop or drifting out to sea during a spectacular sunset.

It is remarkable how difficult it is for us to really to see ourselves in our death scenes. What we described is the scene, not ourselves dying. We, often, seem to remove ourselves from the scene. This reflects an understandable resistance to imagining ourself as old or actually dying.

For those who work with the dying, a critically related question is *"How can we be at home in the face of the great suffering we are called to witness?"* Dying people are remarkably sensitive to the emotional states of people around them. Our anxieties and fears are highly contagious. Mercifully, so also is both peace and love.

5

MICROTUBULE

MOON TRIGRAM

HISTORIC CONTEXT— *In the 1970s, both the terms ESP and "hypnosis were not part of the normal medical community. That has changed over the years, with hypnosis now becoming a preferred form of therapy. There are now schools for Certification and States with their own "rules and regulations."*

This is still not true yet with extrasensory perception (ESP). But that will be next, as the enteric nervous system has now been described. Research is now suggesting our gut is a second brain, and primary for thoughts and feelings. It would necessarily become part of any super soldier program around intuition and hunches.

The historic context was that both instincts and intuition (lunar) could become powerful tools for use in our limits of perception. Hypnosis could span beyond space and time (past life regression), and allow "paranormal" access to critical decision-making power tools. It was a first *gate to the subconscious, and the* Non-Local Mind.

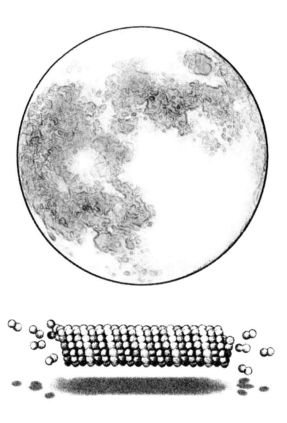

Chapter Five

ESP & Self-Hypnosis

Time is a duration of consciousness. It is the way we organize memories.

–ROBERT ORNSTEIN [*The Psychology of Consciousness*]

Seal Corporation

In the late Fall of 1971, I was contacted by Ted Krueger of Seal Corporation (Amherst, Massachusetts). Seal Corporation was very interested in work being done with extra-sensory perception (ESP) by the Organization for the Advancement of Knowledge, Inc. (O.A.K.). O.A.K. had already developed into a "think-tank" for the Boeing Aircraft Company (to also include Battelle Northwest, and Douglas United Nuclear) in 1970. By 1972, it grown into a large research group with a course I'd taught called Paraphysics (Natural Sciences) which was part of the Experimental College at the University of Washington.

O.A.K., Inc. developed out of that set of classes with more than 450 people taking the course in Paraphysics over a 12-week period. Other schools, included Evergreen Experimental College and three regional Community Colleges, began offered this very popular course. From there, a number of the students wanted to go further by doing some actual study in the paranormal field. Most of the members were graduate students or had been part of other think-tanks prior to O.A.K.'s invitation.

Basically, Seal Corp. wanted to build supermen whose skills were verging on the paranormal. Their first project on ESP was to develop a subjective screening questionnaire geared toward those whose ability with guessing (ESP) was beyond normal inference. Normal inference, also known as standard deviation, is defined as 50% for guessing the flip of a coin. The questionnaire was developed to help identify those individuals who were in the top 2% (over normal inference) and worthy of possible further training.

The next assignment for O.A.K. from Seals Corp. (later evolving into the Navy Seal program), was to develop a model which could be used to train the top 2% of individuals, discovered through the subjective questionnaire, and then fine tune their abilities in guessing. At the same time, Dr. Milan Ryzl, the pioneer in Czechoslovakian Paraphysics, defected in 1967 to the United States.

Due to OAK's ongoing work with ESP, Dr. Milan Ryzl was eventually brought into my home for interviews and debriefing on his work with ESP. During that period of Cold War, the Soviet Union supported and developed Paraphysical research. They wanted a new direction in weapons that would exploit anomalous human potential.

In the late 60's, a series of papers (including the *Journal of Paraphysics*, Paraphysical Laboratory, Downton, England) were being prepared on the state of Paraphysics in the Iron Curtain countries of Europe. These were part of the *Symposium of Psychotronics* with the editorial board changing each year. The early editor, from 1967 to 1970, was B. Herbert. Then, in 1971 it was Zdenek Rejdak, and then Victor Adamenko in 1972.

These papers were comprised of hundreds of pages and discussed such topics as telepathy, telekinesis, and precognition as well as the other areas commonly referred to as Extra Sensory phenomena (ESP for "inside the body" and PK for "outside the body"). These papers can be viewed at www.earthpulse.com under the "Mind Effects" section of that site. Several years later (1971), Ostrander and Schroeder reviewed these studies in their classic *Psychic Discoveries behind the Iron Curtin.*

Dr. Milan Ryzl, a biochemist at the Czech Institute of Biology in Prague, had spent years (1950's) trying to interest his government in supporting psychic research during the period when Communists ruled Czechoslovakia. By the early 60's, interest in parapsychology was tolerated. His studies involved hypnotic techniques for developing ESP subjects. To demonstrate these techniques, Ryzl used his psychic subjects to predict the winning numbers in the Czech public lottery which was successful three weeks in a row.

Early ESP Studies

From historical and current research in ESP studies, it now appears "as if" extrasensory information is a kind of coordinate shifting in they way man assimilates information. This, then, shifts our perspectives and concepts of on-going reality (like asking a question instead of answering it). Subtle shifts in consciousness actually make a difference in our perception of "what is happening."

Some very important experiences came out in our studies with ESP during the Apollo 14 Mission studies with Edgar Mitchell. He was devoted to the studies of ESP and made demands to conduct several experiments when he was in space.

One of the most important experiments in the study of ESP happened during the Apollo 14 Mission when Edgar Mitchell was placed on the moon and did some extensive extrasensory studies with Olaf Johnson. Johnson, at the time, was a fairly reputable medium (psychic) from Chicago. How these studies became part of NASA's program is another story.

The Apollo Mission was so far in space that we now had a time where we could measure events accurately as to whether they were happening at the speed of light, faster than the speed of light or instantaneously. These studies were so important that they became secret. Our whole concept of what an altered state of consciousness was took on an entirely different framework than previous models.

We did a number of experiments to determine some of the basic physical criteria on extrasensory perception. Because the moon was a further distance than anyone could travel on earth, and the fact that there was a vacuum in space, time was able to become a measurable quantity in a vacuum.

Light, for example, was known to travel at a different speed in air (or water) than it did in a vacuum. In this case, it took light 1.8 seconds to travel from the moon to the earth. One of the experiments, then, was to measure the time it took an extrasensory image to travel through space (in a vacuum).

Using very sophisticated methodologies, including Cesium clocks and the like, it was found that the time taken for an ESP communication from the Moon to Earth was completely independent of time. Extrasensory perception was, essentially, instantaneous to all practical purposes and appeared to be completely independent of time.

The second set of experiments demonstrated that ESP communication was completely independent of distances. Studies from the far side of the moon, to those in front of the moon, showed no differences. More importantly, ESP did not seem to obey the one over R-square law often used in Physics at the time.

This old law basically states that there will be an exponential drop in signal strength by the radius or distance (Newton) the further you are away from a signal. This was not found true with ESP. It had no drop in signal strength to distance. ESP was not only independent of time; it was also independent of space (or distance).

Psi energy, what we call the psionic field for ESP, appears to be completely independent of time. The third set of experiments conducted was, essentially, to send a transmission through the earth. The results showed no deterioration of signal indicating that ESP transmissions were independent of mass.

Some Basic Definition Used In ESP

Now we have the problem of defining what extrasensory perception really is and how man might be able to use it. Traditionally, the field of ESP studies has divided these phenomena into two ways it is observed in nature. The first is called extrasensory perception (ESP), dealing primarily with the mind (or 'inside' the body).

The second type of observed phenomena is known as Psychokinesis or PK phenomena (taking place 'outside' the body). Poltergeist, apportation (the materialization and dematerialization of matter), and levitation, all fall under the category of psychokinetic phenomena. In PK, the mind appears to be causing changes in the physical environment.

In ESP, a mind is involved with another mind, or itself. All aspects take place within the body, and not the environment. With this definition ESP is then subdivided into five major categories. The first is called clairvoyance; the second is telepathy; the third is called astral projection; the fourth is precognition; and the fifth is what is generally called "occult radar" or radiathesisia.

Clairvoyance is the phenomena whereby your being is located in one spot and you receive information about something that may be happening someplace else. This information can be "perceived" in a variety of forms. It can appear as "clairvoyant," where you 'see' something happening; "Clair-audience," where you 'hear' something; or even "clair-sension," where you 'feel' something happening.

It should be remembered that all of this extrasensory perception is brought into your consciousness via some form of hallucination. In this case, I define hallucination as data received through one or all of your five senses, but independent of them; not caused by any of your five senses. In other words, you did not actually "see" the aura, but this is how it was "communicated" to your consciousness.

As an aside, for those interested in such concepts as "auras," what is generally happening is easily explained within these definitions. For example, the way the cones and rods in your eye work it is possible to see "rings of light" around another body (human or inanimate). With some effort, an Eastern world-view, and imagination, it is quite possible to determine the emotional state of another.

You have this information already in the subconscious. It might be from some subtle body movements (body language), or an even unexplained resource. Now once observed, how does this information somehow gravitate from the deeper levels of consciousness (subconscious or unconscious part of self) to normal awareness?

Since consciousness is derived from inputs to one of the normal five senses, communication has you "seeing" it as a ring of colors. But, it did not actually derive from this modality. Once one becomes aware of the associated colors to various modalities of consciousness, we can then use this technique to relate more subtle depths of insight to ongoing moods and their shifts.

Astral projection is where your physical being is in one place and your consciousness is someplace else, like down the street observing something going on at that location. The most important thing to realize is that a coordinate shift has occurred. The information you receive through using clairvoyance and astral projection is basically the same, with the real difference between the two is how you experience receiving the information.

What is happening here is that you have shifted a coordinate system in your consciousness in the way you are assimilating the information. A good first book on this subject would be Journeys out of Body, by Robert Monroe. Torrens and Kerrington have also written books on astral projection.

One can actually study astral projection with subjects under hypnosis, mentally guiding their consciousness into the next room and then asking them to describe it. The Rosicrucians have a very interesting exercise which teaches us how to look at things in reality, without space separating one thing from another.

One way is to get up next to a telephone pole and then peek around it until you can see the next telephone pole down the street. Do this, while not being able to see the space between the two poles. That's just about an accurate way of looking at reality as the way you are "seeing it" at this moment. It is very subjective and limited, but you can now see how the two telephone poles are, in the strictest sense of the word, "connected."

Now, what is the relationship between precognition and clairvoyance? Precognition is clairvoyance with time being the variable. Precognition is seeing events which take place in the future. Retrognition sees things that have happened in the past. The Chicago police have used Olaf Johnson to locate objects that have been lost. Precognition and retrognition are, therefore, the same phenomena with different time coordinates.

What is the difference between clairvoyance and telepathy? In clairvoyance, for example, information from one location is received in another, by you, for example. In telepathy, information is sent from one spot (like you), to another. The difference is in which direction the information is going and whether it is being consciously sent or simply perceived.

Radiathesisia is the use of a foreign object, something "outside" the body, to communicate information to your consciousness. Water witching, or the use of a dowsing rod to locate underground springs or wells, is an example of radiathesisia. A healer may use a pendulum to swing over the body of a patient to locate illness.

The healer is using a foreign object to communicate information back to his consciousness; he is displaying radiathesisia or "occult radar." Dr. Macbeth, in London (Oxford), has done some serious work in this field. Another example would be the use of the I-Ching or tarot cards. All are classified as forms of radiathesisia.

Hypnosis and its Relationship to ESP

The standard definitions used for hypnosis often state that hypnosis is a borderline state between sleeping and waking. Any state characterized by an intense concentration of attention in one area, accompanied by a profound lack of attention in other areas, may also be considered hypnosis. With this type of definition, everyone is considered to be continuously in a light state of hypnosis.

The depth of hypnosis, which is an implied issue in this definition, may be defined as the difference between the intensity of concentration in one sphere or area and the depth of inhibition in others. Attention focused in one area creates a corresponding lacuna, or lack of attention, in other areas of the brain. Deeper states of hypnosis are created by centering the attention for prolonged periods.

With these technical definitions of hypnosis, a useful scientific model for relating hypnosis to extra sensory perception is now possible.

Postulate I: Focused attention - intensity. *The conscious experience is associated with the nervous processes which take place outside of a certain critical level of awareness/alertness. This function, defined as I(c), or intensity of concentration, varies considerably in a state of hypnosis when attention is focused.*

Postulate II: Energy. *Psi Energy, arbitrarily defined as E(psi), is an equivalent in the field of extra-sensory phenomenon of what, in our three-dimensional world, is called energy.*

Correlate A: *E(psi) is not limited by time.*

Correlate B: *E(psi) cannot be transformed into other known physical energies (example: heat into light).*

Correlate C: *E(psi) operates by manipulating the transformation of physical energies.*

Postulate III: *Psi Energy is responsible for extra-sensory perception and psycho-kinetic phenomenon (PK).*

Postulate IV: *Psi Energy is the product of some aspect of the metabolic processes.*

Physical data regarding the relationship between metabolic processes and extra-sensory perception can be found in the book *"Beyond Telepathy"* by Andrija Puharich.

Postulate V: *The generation of the Psi Energy rapidly decreases the level of alertness. This immediately explains:*

(1) why each conscious act has a limited duration,

(2) why we experience a permanent train of changing thoughts, and

(3) why our attention permanently shifts from one object or thought to

   the next.

When we think, *Psi Energy* is created. *The Psi Energy automatically decreases the level of alertness so that our attention shifts to something else.*

Postulate VI: *The intensity of conscious experience or concentration, I(c), depends on the time rate of the generation of Psi Energy. Mathematically, this is described as follows:*

$$dE(psi)/dt = A(e) \times I(c)$$

What this means is that the rate of change of *E(psi)* as a function of time *(dE(psi)/dt)*, also known as an organ of concentration, is equal to some geographical constant, A(e), times the intensity of concentration, I(c).

More simply stated, *Psi Energy [E(psi)]* is equal to a geographical constant times the intensity of concentration, I(c), times the amount of time that the thought is held as shown below:

$$E(psi) = A(e) \times I(c) \times t$$

If we cannot make any particular thought last long enough, it should be sufficient to repeat it again and again until the value of the individual brief periods add up to a sufficient value. The equation now becomes as follows:

$$E(psi) = A(e) \times I(c) \times [t(1) + t(2) + t(3) + ...]$$

Discussion

Extra-sensory perception is often observed in hypnosis, a state characterized by a single intensive thought. Recurrent cases of psycho-kinetic phenomena, such as the haunted-house variety, are often reported to be connected with previous tragic events associated with intensity of concentration, I(c).

The frequently reported cases of crisis telepathy - ESP contact between two persons, one of who is dying or in grave danger - are necessarily associated with intense thought or concentration. The length of time experienced depends entirely upon the circumstances.

The discovery of mental impregnation, known in the literature as psychometry, gave evidence that repeated identical thoughts increased the expected psychic effect. Wearing a ring for a long time will "imprint" memory of the wearer onto the ring, however, just quickly slipping a ring on and then off and handing it to a Psychometrist will not generally yield any memory of the wearer.

Religious tradition asserts that repeated prayers may be more effective than a single one. In other words, the more you repeat the same prayer, or the more you do a single ritual, the greater the effect. Along these same lines, "tithing" might be seen as consisting of one's time or attention rather than the traditional meaning of money to the Church. Many eastern religions, for example, require more than ten percent of your life (2.5 hours each day) in meditation.

> **Postulate VII:** *The formation of Psi Energy, which is created by a mental act, preserves the semantic content of the thought which created it.*

In essence, your thought is uniquely distinct. If you deviate from your thought slightly, it is a different thought-form.

The stimulating action of Psi formation on the brain may account for memory, more particularly, active recollection. The influence of Psi formation increases the level of awareness of the neuro-patterns corresponding to the thought to be remembered. This corresponding semantic content is, then, consciously re-experienced.

Method of Induction:

When questioning or desiring thoughts are intense enough, lasting long enough, or repeated frequently enough, the organ of *Psi Energy* is produced ($dE(psi)/dt$) in sufficient intensity and structuring to be able to cause a detectable effect in the physical world. This may occur in hypnotic states, in states of elated or fearful emotions, or when interest, motivation, or desire is strongly increased.

Therefore, the ideal process of extra-sensory perception works in this manner. We begin with a simple chart with *Level of Awareness* plotted against *Level of Alertness* (Figure 1). Anything below this line is not realized as a conscious thought, while everything above the line is consciously experienced.

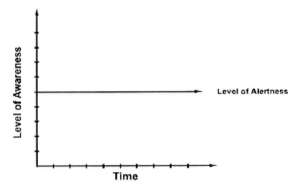

Figure 1

We, then, form an intense desire or question in our conscious mind that we wish to have occur, happen, or know (be given an answer to). This must first come into being as a normal, but intense, thought form or question. This is the individual confronting the continuum. It is this question or thought that creates an organ of Psi Energy (Figure 2).

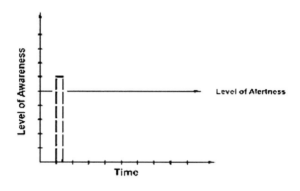

Figure 2

This can be described as a "lump" of information. The graph of Figure 2 shows that "lump" to be about a 1/3 unit of time. If the thought can be held for a more prolonged period of time, this will increase the intensity of concentration [I(c)], making the "lump" broader (more area under the curve), and most importantly, above a critical level of awareness.

The sharpness of this thought is depicted by a square-edged "lump." This is where one thought-form varies from another. It also defines the precision of your request or the difference between one set of Psi Energy production and another.

Consciousness is then dropped into a "blank mind" state (Figure 3). Note that there is no conscious awareness in this state of mind. It is quite unique and quite different than the one used to create an organ of *Psi Energy*.

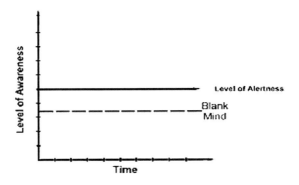

Figure 3

The actual visualization aspect is to see this event as a "switch," going from the idea itself or question, to a specific void state. What eventually occurs is that this information is impressed onto consciousness as a vision or an event occurrence (Figure 4).

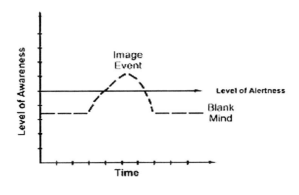

Figure 4

This event, to the thinker, is independent of both space and time. The usual duration of time for this to become clear and aware can take upward of two minutes or more depending, mostly, on how clean the "blank mind" state is held.

In actuality, however, what really occurs is - the question being asked is not intense enough to impress itself onto the conscious state (Figure 5).

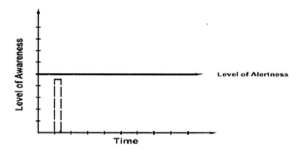

Figure 5

Lacking in intensity, the block of energy or, more precisely, block of information that is created is small. Thus, the Psi Energy output is minimal, if any at all (Figure 6). When people drop themselves into trance states, they are generally not in a "blank mind" state. There are a lot of subconscious thoughts going on even as they are going down into the trance state.

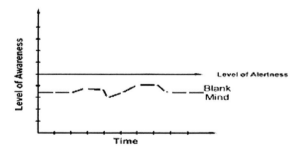

Figure 6

All of these subconscious thoughts are on a subliminal level, not experienced in a conscious form. The person may not even be aware of them since most of us have no training or discipline to hold onto the "blank mind" state for any length of time. This is the Zen form of the "no mind" state.

This is a place where most meditation, as a discipline, attempts to go. The best way to begin to do this is by visualizing a "white light" at the third eye (center of the forehead). What happens next is that thoughts begin to disappear and a calming feeling sweeps over the body, not unlike day-dreaming. One is not conscious of thoughts or forms. This state is often associated with light alpha brainwaves.

Consequently, the information path gets distorted and a weird pattern emerges. This vision of information, or event experience, is distorted (Figure 7)

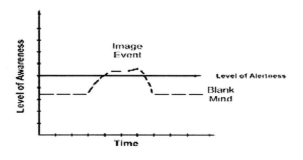

Figure 7

Prototaxic, or trance modes, of consciousness are characterized by loss of ego known as trance states of consciousness. It is considered the lowest state of awareness as most who go into this place often do not remember their experience. This is often associated with shamanistic forms of consciousness. A deeper discussion on this subject can be found in the books, *"ESP Induction Through Forms Of Self-Hypnosis"* and its sequel *"Power Tools For The 21st Century."*

Higher forms of the trance state include art (*Parataxic mode*) and creativity (*Syntaxic mode*). *Parataxic* experience consists of relationships with images whose meaning remains on the symbolic level. *Syntaxic* experiences occur when the conscious ego cooperates willingly with the subconscious. Charles Honorton's term for this state was *"syntactic,"* but John Curtis Gowan's ontology of mystical states of consciousness is more complete. Here, meaning is fully cognized with minimal distortion in the production of *Psi Energy*.

Older magical ceremonies such as the Banishing Ritual and Middle Pillar exercise can be seen as designed to facilitate higher forms of concentration (i.e. Syntaxic mode). Other ways of obtaining this experience are biofeedback, meditation, peak experiences, higher *Jhana* (again, Gowan's term) states of yoga, and so on. The Banishing Ritual provides protection from invading thoughts and distractions. Concentration during this form of ritual purification is intense, structured, and prolonged.

The magical concept of "energized enthusiasm," arousing one's self emotionally, seems to be pertinent to facilitating telepathic reception. Puharich believes reception is improved by "parasympathetic activation" in which there is an increase in released acetylcholine, a brain neuro-transmitter. He also holds that the telepathic sending of information is easier when there is an increased amount of adrenaline in the system.

These metabolic processes need not be viewed as "causal," but as simultaneous or synchronous with the ESP experience. This way of viewing the body metaphorically is the bases for modern alchemy - the process of personal transformation. Psi meaning comes through intense visual, auditory, and kinesthetic psycho-sensory experiences.

Summary of the Protocol:

A simple method for inducing extra-sensory perception through forms of self-hypnosis is now given as:

> (1) **Formulate the question.**
> (2) **Hold that thought for as long as possible.**
> (3) **Assume that the event has occurred.**
> (4) **Drop into a "blank mind" state and wait.**

When questioning or desirous thoughts are intense enough, lasting long enough or repeated frequently enough, psi is produced in sufficient intensity and structure to be detectable in the physical world. This may occur in hypnotic states, in states of intentionality, elated or traumatic emotions, or when interest, motivation, or desire is strongly increased.

The individual confronts the continuum with desire and prolonged concentration. The question being asked must be intense enough to impress itself on the unconscious. Lacking intensity, the signal will not be perceived. Intentionality strengthens the signal path.

Consciousness is then dropped into a "blank" state, an empty state, or "beginner's mind." The actual visualization is a switch from the concentrated point to the void. When this occurs the information is impressed on consciousness resulting in a psychophysical perceptual event. This event is independent of both space and time.

Ordinarily, when people spontaneously fall into trance states, they are generally not in a "blank mind" state of expectant emptiness. There is a chatter of subconscious thoughts going on even as the process deepens toward sleep. These thoughts are generated and go on automatically at a subliminal level, often without awareness.

Consequently, the information or signal path gets distorted and weird patterns emerge, much like those experienced in dreams. In a waking dream, distorted signals may be perceived as "spirit guides," automatic handwriting, or other autonomous related phenomena of trance states.

This research into ESP has yielded incredible results and offered conclusions that are more far reaching than might first be realized. It may well be that man is not looking into the future via ESP, but creating it with his own belief systems and values. To suggest that one could predict something 400 times beyond normal inference is to also suggest a more fundamental possibility.

The brain itself can be seen as a four dimensional hologram of 5-space. This concept is part of a holographic model of the universe and may suggest a non-local mind aspect not yet described in the literature. Rather than see the universe as quantized, it may in fact be about information and the resolution of information. This is how a holographic universe might be constructed.

Predicated on what part of the brain is being used for conscious awareness might suggest access to other realities. By changing what part of the brain is being used at any given moment might allow a different "movie" to be experienced as "real." The intensity of concentration and "blank mind" states suggest the possibility of a broader definition of the "mind."

To suggest that other states of awareness could offer access to other realities might become a valuable tool toward consciousness evolution. The study of ESP is just a brief beginning journey toward the development of simple tools for true transformation and the evolution of man's consciousness.

The World's First Psychic Tournament

On September 21, 1975, Llewellyn Publications sponsored the World's First Psychic Tournament in Minneapolis, MN as part of their 5th Annual Gnosticon Festival. The tournament itself was co-sponsored by the Foundation for the Study of Man, originally set up to continue the work of Dr. Rhine and his work in ESP at Duke University. Many famous psychics were invited, including such personalities as John Pierrakos and Sibyl Leek.

The author of this paper was also invited to test the proposed models for inducing ESP ability using forms of self-hypnosis. Since he was relatively unknown for having any abilities in this ESP field, it seemed to hold some potential as a valid first study. More than 20 nationally known psychics also participated at this event.

The clairvoyance test consisted of twenty (20) cards randomly pulled from ten (10) poker decks. Each participant was to guess the suit of each card. With one chance in four of guessing the correct suit, the average score for a run of 20 cards with no ESP ability is 5. Each participant was given five (5) different runs. A final score determined the winner, with a total of 25 representing the norm.

What happened is now history: More than 50 percent of those participating showed normal scores ranging from 22 to 27 out of a possible 100. Most of the more well-known psychics showed some paranormal ability in clairvoyance, as expected, with total scores averaging between 8 and 12 correct answers out of 20. One well known psychic even had a score as high as 61 out of a total possible 100.

Using the technique of ESP induction through forms of self-hypnosis as outlined in this paper, however, Richard Alan Miller did not have a single run less than 16 out of twenty. His total score was 83 out of 100, more than two orders of magnitude greater probability than scores of nationally recognized psychics (Figure 9).

Of course, this does not constitute a proof of this model. What it does represent, however, is a need to understand the true significance of what self-hypnosis is and how it relates to extra-sensory perception (ESP). Something definitely made a difference in the performance of what is defined as clairvoyance. How might this be applied to therapy? Or even to such questions as to the role of placebo, the belief that you can do something beyond your scope.

Chapter Two addresses the nature and importance of attitude as a prerequisite for improved clairvoyance performance. The goal was to create a subjective screening questionnaire.

The Mind Room Exercise

> "I am entering a solemn house. It is called 'the house of inner composure or self collection.' In the background are many burning candles arranged so as to form four pyramid-like points. An old man stands at the door of the house. People enter, they do not talk and often stand still in order to concentrate. The old man at the door tells me about the visitors to the house and says: 'When they leave they are pure.' I enter the house now, and am able to concentrate completely."
>
> C. G. JUNG, MEMORIES, DREAMS, REFLECTIONS, 1961

A "mind room" is a place of many functions, a safety zone to which you can retreat, or catch your breath. It can restore your Spirit and gear you up for action. It is a place in which your mind, in an altered state of consciousness, can deal with a problem that might otherwise seem insurmountable in the normal state of reality.

Preparation:

It is very easy to reach this sanctuary. Sit comfortably in a chair, or lie in a bed, and then close your eyes. Once you have gone to this special place, you may be able to go there with your eyes open. Relax every muscle in your body, beginning with the top of your head, working your way down the body to the tips of your toes.

While you are doing this, count backward from ten to zero. Tell yourself that, on reaching zero, you will be in a very deep state of relaxation. This will be a threshold for an altered state of consciousness.

You may feel a tingling in your fingers and a fluttering in your eyelids. These are signs that you are now passing through the door into a state of heightened awareness in which you can tap into the dormant powers of your mind.

Now the fluttering of the transition has passed, as you have penetrated deeper and deeper into the recesses of your mind.

The Exercise:

You are in a very pleasant, deeply relaxed state now, basking in a drowsy sense of semi-reality, even though you are perfectly aware of the world around you - the muted noise from next door, or perhaps the sound of silence emanating from a snow-covered or sun-baked street, and the ticking of your clock. You know that you can return to this world at any moment you wish by simply opening your eyes.

But you don't wish to return just yet. You continue to allow the half-formed thoughts and images to drift around in your head, until you come to a small, cozy, comfortable room where you feel completely safe and secure. This room is your safety zone, your retreat. Whenever you enter this room, you will at once feel secure and content.

All fears and apprehensions are securely locked outside, once you have entered this island of safety and closed the door. The very creak of the hinges herald this, the click of the lock which you bolt against intrusion confirms it. Any problem that seems overwhelming before will be easily solved here.

The room is small and intimate, furnished exactly to your taste. It contains your favorite armchair. It is deeply upholstered shape, and supportive, its sturdy bulk protective. The floor is softly carpeted, so that you can walk or pace in relaxed comfort.

The drawn drapes that cover the windows deaden the noise of the outside world and allow only a soft light to filter through. Although you are alone in your room, this calm solitude is filled with an exhilarating sense of space and freedom. Fears, cares, discomfort have no place here. Your room is the home of well-being, where you breathe in a security free from all uncertainty. Your room is the home of your real and best self.

Here you can safely settle down and rest until you are strong enough to emerge and confront the outside world again. Here you can let your expanded mind range over any problem you have. The room will coax your mind toward a solution, gently, slowly, surely, inevitably.

All you need do to return to ordinary consciousness is to tell yourself that you will now count slowly from one to three. At the count of three you will open your eyes. As soon as you do, you will be fully awake, and completely relaxed and unafraid, capable of dealing efficiently with whatever problem confronts you.

A Critical Decision-Making Power-Tool

The implications of having access to paranormal abilities (like ESP), through the use of hypnosis, are staggering. This would suggest that altered states of consciousness (ASC) allow access to a universe which is beyond space and time. That universe is more about information and its resolutions - how information enfolds inward or outward in detail.

Magick has been defined as "the art of changing consciousness at will." Our thoughts (and fears) create those realities. The nature of a thought-form, and how psyche become matter, will be found in the depth of hypnosis. By repeating a thought-form (via ritual) again and again, we then allow it to happen. That is why persistence is often considered superior to genius.

By thinking with the "gut," a more timeless set of answers become available. When one tends to think about something, often options also are created (like chess). This is why consciousness is considered so limited. Once options are created, doubts set in. And then, *it becomes a self fulfilling prophesy.*

To be able to listen to your inner gut will provide the highest level of information and survival. This is why this set of protocols is now taught to almost everyone at the Naval Academy. They allow for responses and accuracies beyond statistical probability and the more limited states associated with consciousness.

6

HOLOGRAPHIC

FIRE TRIGRAM

HISTORICAL CONTEXT – *Like the serpent power of Tantric Yoga, it was realized that more was going on inside the body than just biochemistry.* The Biological Function of the Third Eye *(1975) outlined a protocol on how to regenerate true nerve tissue, using just visualization exercises. That became a protocol, using a visualization of the chill up the spine.*

Archetypes became a way of seeing how something might go (bigger picture), and be incorporated into possible outcome scenarios. This gave a second validation to merging hunches and gut feelings. Mythologies allowed more human element identification, and then offered stories – with endings.

The historic context then is about identifying a specific myth you might be enacting, and how it must end. It gives a way to see how things might go, when following a certain story line. Using Greek Mythology there are only 22 Big Stories in the City *(Tarot).*

Chapter Six

Archetypal Encounters
& Mythical Living

WITH IONA MILLER, AS CO-AUTHOR

"...to behave is to choose one pattern among many."

−PROFESSOR JOSE M.R. DELGADO, MADRID

We all encounter forces and behavior patterns which seem beyond our capacity to understand or control. We say and do things we never believed we were capable of, and then claim we "must have been beside ourselves." Our subconscious minds provoke us into behavior we would never consciously choose otherwise.

At first glance, each individual's problems, experiences, and innate qualities seem unique. Yet, from another perspective, we all share the common inheritance of a mythic dimension of life which psychologist Carl Jung termed the "collective unconscious." This is where the so-called Tarot cards depict the *"28 different stories in the big city."* [SEE EXERCISE D]

All of our human potential for both "good" and "evil" comes from this subconscious source. It reveals itself through dreams, visions, art, fantasy, imagination, and myths or tales of all cultures. These themes and myths contain a value far greater than their creative or literary merits. Not only do myths in-form us of the origins of thought and philosophy, they also reveal an ancient, sacred dimension of human experience.

Active Imagination

The realm of the collective unconscious is "populated" with mythical figures which are described as gods and goddesses. Each has a retinue of corresponding moods, landscapes, personality traits, and preferences. These figures personify man's qualities or modes of being in the world. Each has particular characteristics. Knowledge of these characteristics or styles can enhance our personal journeys of self-discovery.

Through personally discovering these gods within ourselves, we gain access to a deeper understanding of both ourselves and others. We all share the journey of self-exploration, even though different aspects of it appear to each of us. Certain of the gods and goddesses may play a major or dominant role in our lives and those of our loved ones, but our Imagination (psyche) contains them all. The more of these basic patterns of life we have access to, the greater our experience of this mythic dimension of life which makes our conscious day-to-day lives even more meaningful.

The realization of our personal potential has often been considered a "key" to life's meaning. To realize the fullness of one's personality and to develop our native abilities and personal characteristics to the highest degree possible is a worthy long-range goal.

Active imagination includes consciousness journeys deep into the psyche, identification, and internal dialogues with personified archetypes. It is a way of building experiential relationships with archetypal forces — harmonizing and honoring them. These internal dialogues can be useful, revealing the autonomous dynamics at work in our lives. These relationships reveal the meaningfulness behind the many complications in our modern lives.

The more we approach our individual wholeness, through expanding our awareness and experiences, the more we are likely to encounter these divine principles from the realm of imagination. This journey toward wholeness is easier to integrate into daily life with a psychological framework for containing and accommodating a wide range of images, emotions, moral views, styles of thought, and even dress.

When we know the characteristics of the various archetypes, we find them reflected back to our consciousness from the environment. We can learn to view their effects on our lives directly and gain in personal, social, and spiritual freedom. If we fail to become consciously aware of their effects, their spontaneous activation may produce devastating effects on the personality. They can create internal divisions in the psyche which may lead to the disintegration of personality. This can result in disease, self-destructive behavior, or even culminate in death.

As we mature into adults, many of us are forced by environmental factors to travel roads which do not follow our natural predispositions. This may create conflicts or crises in our lives which require either change or understanding. Some of us are forced, for example, to work in occupations which do not really suit our personalities. For some this becomes a challenge to be met and accepted; others of us just feel like "square pegs in round holes."

The Concept of Archetypes

The work of Swiss psychologist Carl Gustav Jung (1875-1961) is becoming of greater and greater interest to the general public. The growing interest in Jungian Psychology (or Depth Psychology) stems from the fact that it answers the needs of many people as a means for relating to "internal" as well as "external" reality. These people are seeking a fuller understanding of the meaning of life in such areas as dreams, fantasy, compulsive behaviors, and self-exploration or enrichment.

The main focus of Jung's work stressed the search for meaning and the development of Individuation, psychological wholeness, or integrity of the personality. Jungian therapy opened the door to the collective unconscious for many, not only to their subconscious desires and motivations, but also to their higher spiritual aspirations and potentials.

Jungian psychology describes the meaning of the symbols and events on the spiritual quest for self-actualization in non-religious terms. It is extremely useful for self-analysis. By gaining a working knowledge of our various facets and how they interrelate, an integration or synthesis of personality becomes possible. This results in high well-being and increased creativity.

In practical terms, Jungian therapy includes developing the awareness of internal guiding principles or Archetypes. We don't need a personal therapist to discover these archetypes within. We can discover them within ourselves if we know what to look for during periods of reflection or introspection.

Archetypes are an innate, or in-born pattern, which function as the underlying matrix behind any event. They are not necessarily transmitted through our genes, but they are fundamental to our method of perceiving nature, god, and man. They are the very substance of our experience of life.

Archetypes may be seen as embodiments of specific functions and their characteristic patterns may be personified by giving each a name. In this way, we can learn to recognize archetypes when they appear in our lives affecting styles of behavior, thought, emotions, attitudes, and dress. Through identifying and naming them, we can take up a meaningful relationship with these characters of our internal world.

The Jungian perspective sees the human perception of "reality" as originating in a projection from an internal motivating factor (archetype) onto our environment. Since we do not perceive the universe of experience directly, but through the filters of our senses, we experience archetypes through sight, touch, taste, smell, and sound.

They also appear through the human functions of feeling, sensation, intuition, and thinking. They are constantly maneuvering our human lives as if we were puppets. In the ancient past, when these powers of the archetypes over the human will were dramatic, or negative, this phenomenon was termed "possession" and it could be demonic or spiritual in nature.

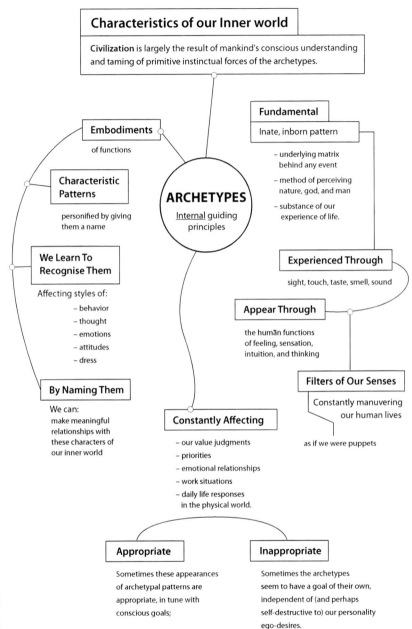

Characteristics of our Inner world

Civilization is largely the result of mankind's conscious understanding and taming of primitive instinctual forces of the archetypes.

Fundamental

Inate, inborn pattern

– underlying matrix behind any event

– method of perceiving nature, god, and man

– substance of our experience of life.

Embodiments

of functions

Characteristic Patterns

personified by giving them a name

ARCHETYPES

Internal guiding principles

We Learn To Recognise Them

Affecting styles of:

– behavior
– thought
– emotions
– attitudes
– dress

Experienced Through

sight, touch, taste, smell, sound

Appear Through

the human functions of feeling, sensation, intuition, and thinking

Filters of Our Senses

Constantly manuvering our human lives

as if we were puppets

By Naming Them

We can: make meaningful relationships with these characters of our inner world

Constantly Affecting

– our value judgments
– priorities
– emotional relationships
– work situations
– daily life responses in the physical world.

Appropriate

Sometimes these appearances of archetypal patterns are appropriate, in tune with conscious goals;

Inappropriate

Sometimes the archetypes seem to have a goal of their own, independent of (and perhaps self-destructive to) our personality ego-desires.

MIND MAP: ELLEYNE KASE

157

On a more common level, archetypes are constantly affecting our value judgments, priorities, emotional relationships, work situations, and daily life responses in the physical world. Sometimes these appearances of archetypal
patterns are appropriate, in tune with conscious goals; but sometimes the
archetypes seem to have a goal of their own, independent of (and perhaps
self-destructive to) our personality ego-desires.

Civilization is largely the result of mankind's conscious understanding and
taming of primitive instinctual forces of the archetypes. With fewer and fewer
"taboos" to control our society, we need to understand our own emotional
upheavals so that we are not overwhelmed by them. We can evolve to an understanding of our subtle and not-so-subtle inner urges, in which case they
cease to compel us and begin to work on our behalf. Thus, we grow out of
counter-productive behaviors into the ability to actualize our highest goals.

For example, if *Aphrodite's* desire for immediate sexual gratification crops up
in our workplace, trouble is likely to follow. That is, trouble will follow if we
are unconsciously compelled into actions we might later regret. But we can
learn to "see through" these impulses, in which case, they lose their compulsive quality.

We might take up an internal dialogue with *Aphrodite*, in our imagination, and
find out she has much better things in store for us! She might admit us to some
of the mysteries of the Anima, or soul. And after all, isn't that more intriguing
than getting fired or charged with a sexual harassment suit?

It is these underlying matrix patterns within the psyche which produce the
outer behavior. When we can see that *Archetypes are motivating factors,* it
is also possible to intuit how a knowledge of their particular characteristics
could be useful in understanding the complexities of life.

But, are these gods and goddesses real in the objective sense? Can they really
manipulate our behavior so subtlety without us noticing them? According to
Jung this is true and we all share this condition. Even those trained in these ar-

eas maintain psychological "blind spots" where we fail to see the archetypes moving us.

Jung saw man, not as an isolated individual, but as being linked with the whole of mankind (and mankind's abilities) through the collective unconscious. This unconscious manifests in the multiple forms of gods and goddesses. These figures take different, though analogous, forms in the various mythologies of the world's cultures.

Thus, the goddesses Isis (Egyptian), Artemis (Greek), and Diana (Roman), all share a common essence and use the same lunar symbolism. The same generic form is also behind the Catholic's *Blessed Virgin Mary* and all are derived from the theme of *Celestial Queen*.

These forms, or archetypes, should not be thought of as nouns (things), but rather as semantic metaphors. They represent powers or qualities, but when we personify them, it is "as if" we take up a relationship with another entity. They assume an anthropomorphic form in imagination in order to make a dialogue easier. This dialogical exchange is just a variation of the I-Thou communications of mysticism.

Archetypes represent an "*as if*" reality. Therefore, it is "*as if*" archetypes compel our behavior until we develop this conscious relationship with them. They are constantly calling to us in psychosomatic disorders, through our emotions, in the bedroom or the boardroom. They fill us with aspirations and repulsions, influencing what we think, feel, and do.

We like to believe that we are independent mature adults, but in effect, it is "*as if*" we repeatedly act out these eternal patterns or stories again over and over. They create our attachments or destroy our relationships on a whim, taking over the human aspects of our existence. We may each have our personal histories, but we draw from the common repertoire of archetypal dramas. These themes are chronically repeated every day though, oftentimes, though we wish we had no part in them.

Each archetype has a group of correspondences (symbols or imagery, and moods), or characteristics, which define its appearance and are recurrent. The relationships of eternal archetypes, with one another and to individual mortals, are related in various myths and appear in all the cultures of the world with certain consistent elements.

In the past, these archetypes were recognized as coming from a divine origin, so they were worshipped as gods or goddesses. We "worship" them today when we turn our attention toward them and their effects on us. They exemplify primordial, or fundamental, patterns of existence. They appear nightly in our dreams, often disguised in modern dress.

The personal experience of archetypal energies, or dynamics, is radically different from mere intellectual conceptions of them. This requires a conscious interaction with the subconscious which may be done through active imagination. We each contain all of the gods and goddesses, in potential, at least. As we come to understand ourselves, the entire "cast of characters" will appear before the conscious perspective.

When we realize how they are coming into our daily lives, we realize them within ourselves and this personal discovery adds another dimension to the experience of life. The result is that we find meaning when we are living the myth of the "wounded healer," "jilted lover," or "captain of industry." Then, we aren't merely stereotypes, but are possessed by the divine forces of life. In this way, the sacred dimension enters daily life.

Archetypes underlie our occupations and preoccupations in life. This does not only mean those tasks for which we are paid, but the latent and actualized tendencies that lie within us all. We can go through major life changes when a different archetype seizes us within. We might change lovers, jobs, or locals, not to mention attitudes and goals.

Sometimes these changes are 180 degree turn-arounds. A vocation differs from a job in that there is an "inner calling" to a particular type of work. Archetypes are the motivation behind our feelings of belonging or "a sense of destiny." This "calling" comes from the god which is the core underlying the expression form *follows function*.

For example, a blue-collar worker who wins a million dollars in a lottery may remain in his same social and employment position. But, the money may allow him to pursue a "road not taken." He might, for example, return to college for further training and become a managerial-type. He might even change political parties and social circles.

Given the resources to actualize a different potential, he switched archetypal dominants in the meantime. He changed from the blue collar theme of *Hephaestus* to the white-collared *Zeus*, with the appearance of *Hermes*, luck of the gambler.

Archetypes also affect our personal style, the way we dress, the colors we like, our mannerisms and lifestyles. For example, a person who seems introverted or reflective, dresses mostly in blues and beiges, and lives alone, would be strongly lunar in character, whether male or female. The dominant archetype here is likely the virginal aspect of Artemis, especially if the individual is spiritual or deeply religious. On the other hand, an aggressive, bellicose individual who enjoys the military life or style, could be seen as living under the dominion of Aries, or Mars. Their color would be red.

Do we present ourselves to the world as a radical punk, a conservative three-piece suit type, an erotic fantasy, California "laid back," or a go-getter entrepreneur? Each is its own archetype motivated by a certain god-form. But, we are many of these archetypes at different times or different phases of life. We are versatile as individuals and may display many facets.

Archetypes In Daily Life

Knowledge of the various archetypal forms helps the ego determine what in life is personal and human. And, what is compulsive, acting-out of ancient divine patterns (instinctual in nature). The more we approach our individual wholeness, the more likely we are to encounter these divine principles from the field of archetypal experiences.

We begin to see archetypal forces operating under their own laws in various phases of human life and endeavors. They influence us on personal, social, and national levels. They come in the ever-changing guises of phobias (irrational fears), prejudices, complexes (interference by an archetype or group of archetypes with the conscious personality), and our runaway ego-trips.

They play through our culture in art, literature, and the movies we so frequently view. When seen objectively in stories, we can identify with them or despise them, but when their effects are subjective, we are entirely "carried away."

Archetypes also lie behind fascinations and enchantments of individuals and nations. They produce the phenomena of "love at first sight" and create fads and set trends, or styles, in the recreation and fashion worlds. They can be contagious as in the case of cults, or political and religious movements. The great attraction of sports is also archetypal in nature.

People will go to war and fight to the death as fanatical "true believers" to defend some political or religious principle. The belief system is influenced by the myth behind it. Charismatic leaders capture the projection of leadership through expressing the subconscious desires of the crowd or herd consciousness (like Adolph Hitler or Jim Jones). Activation of these archetypal powers opens the door for both good and evil and creates an arena for the emergence of ethics and morals.

Ultimately, though, self-awareness is a personal matter we should all tackle individually. Self-knowledge benefits society as a by-product by creating transformed individuals who can "make a difference."

Culturally-modified archetypes are behind the modern drive to discover our "roots." These roots are probably physical in that they reflect our genetic heritage. But for some, they are psychological roots, drawn from patterns with which one feels kinship or relatedness. Whatever our belief system, from scientific to religious, rest assured there are a group of archetypal forces behind them.

When we consciously relate to archetypes, they begin to have a personal context or meaningful place in our lives. This enlarges our ability to experience the transpersonal dimension of the psyche or soul. By personification, we come to know the qualities and manifestations of the gods in "digestible chunks." We learn more deeply about them on ever-increasing octaves of experience. Psychic energy (libido) may, therefore, be thought of as *quantized*.

We can begin to see *Hermes, Athena, Zeus*, and *Themes* operating in our lives, even if we can't fully understand the reality they represent. In this perspective, the essential focus on "reality" occurs where inner material is being projected from the unconscious into our environment. This affects our work, relationships, as well as our spiritual transformation or process of changing to become what we aspire toward.

The deep mind manifests through these archetypal patterns, personified as gods and goddesses, communicating messages to the conscious mind. With an awareness of how these patterns recur, it is possible to influence our destiny. Many of us are somewhat self-defeating, or even self-destructive. We could all benefit by understanding archetypal processes. We suffer from our attenuated versions of the archetype. When we are out of proper relationship to the archetypes, we can become "dominated" by them.

It is possible to learn to balance exaggerated dominance by any form through applied *Creative Imagination*. The basic myth-themes represent all kinds of life situations including realities of outer and inner experiences. If the personality is too one-sided, it is possible to revise it by consciously developing the qualities represented by complementary god-forms. This balances the personality and enriches life.

Archetypes - As a Method of Self Analysis

Having integrated ourselves into the outer world, we can enter our inner world by examining our relationships with the archetypes, thus gaining in self-awareness. Archetypes can't always be subjected to intellectual analysis since they can be illusive. Direct experiential contact is more important than analysis. Nevertheless, a conceptual understanding of the range of archetypal manifestations is a useful tool which we acquire through study, reflection, and application of knowledge.

Archetypes represent a paradoxical synthesis of opposites and are, therefore, neither "good" nor "bad" as a prognosis on one's psychological condition. What is desirable is the experience of archetypes, consciously, not any certain archetypes over others.

Each archetype has its values and drawbacks. We seek to know the range of archetypes which are within us when we enter the inner adventure. In this manner we gain in humanity and versatility.

Ultimately, the archetypes appear to synthesize together in the grand reconciling figures of the higher Self which represents our wholeness or illumination. The inner guiding principle of the Self manifests to the conscious mind as the various archetypal forces with their eternal myth-themes or life-patterns.

We know, directly, when we have been touched by an archetype whenever we experience an exaggerated, irrational, over-emotional reaction. When we seem "out of control," it is because we are taken over by the dominating power of the archetype and are temporarily its slave. This affords us the opportunity to discover a layer of ourselves--that which watches this process impassively and objectively - *The Witness*.

Self-analysis gentles some of the unbounded fury of the subconscious by developing understanding between conscious and subconscious drives. Our behavior can only become purposeful and coherent when inner and outer goals harmonize. If we turn our attention inward to the archetypes and consider them valuable, they become our allies or guides.

If we watch ourselves continually for those moments when conscious control breaks down, we get insight into the realm of the gods. Watch what creates enthusiasm, anger, or depression in yourself and others. Try to peer through to the god-form at the core of symptoms and situations. In this manner, we can learn to relate to the play of events from a dispassionate perspective, mellowing over-reactive instinctual tendencies.

We can either be ruled by the archetypes or learn to rule along with them by cooperating with the trends revealed by the psyche. Eventually, the archetypal figures, which began as an arcane concept and seemed like strangers, will become our constant companions and valued friends and advisors.

Some may remain closer to us than others, but all will lie within our spectrum of acquaintance. A sense of inner self-assurance develops and an inner world, every bit as enticing as the physical, becomes ours.

Archetypes – As a Means of Self-Realization

Once we perceive archetypal material manifesting in our life, and can distinguish one archetype from another, our mental imagery comes more sharply into focus. Now the phase of re-integration begins. Archetypes on the inner planes produce a type of quasi-consciousness. They behave as independent partial personalities.

If they are dysfunctional, they come out in our complexes; if they are integrated they appear as transpersonal resources. The model of a pantheon gives us a tool for examining the different facets of our personality, providing various archetypal perspectives on daily living.

The archetypal dominant in a given person's life determines the life-theme most frequently repeated. Archetypes produce behavior patterns. They entrain their corresponding symbols which appear in dream life, fantasy, emotions, thoughts, and behaviors. To attempt to consciously control them with the ego and will is merely a fantasy and may provoke a negative reaction from the subconscious mind. Archetypes act like instincts when they shape the conscious content through motivation and modification.

The images become more subtle as we penetrate the depths of the psyche. They become more fundamental, more primal, more abstract, reflecting very early experience of self. A firm foundation is built through dealing fully with the more easily-grasped images. When one image has been digested sufficiently, its energy or libido flows into activating another archetype. While this sequence is not fixed, an ordering model is a useful tool for studying archetypes. Do not attempt to dash through a meditation on every archetype. Take your time and savor the flavor of each.

When archetypes appear, look for their characteristic sense of fadedness or destiny. If you meditate on a certain archetype, you may, activate certain synchronistic phenomena, or meaningful coincidences. Through the vocabulary of the corresponding symbols and keyword associations, you may notice that particular archetypal patterns are at work in your life. Keep a journal of these observations. In this way a bridge is slowly built, connecting the conscious and unconscious mind.

Once a particular way of looking at reality is established, it automatically sets up limitations or boundary conditions. However, there is great latitude if one has the ability to subjectively choose among many such realities without falling prey to identification with the subconscious powers. Remember, you are all of them together, and more, not only one or another of them, or those of your gender. You can participate as a whole person in your choices rather than being merely compelled by unconscious motivations.

There is more than one way to look at the reality of archetypes operating in our lives. This description of archetypes has been conditioned by the assumption of a hierarchal model. This variation on "Pilgrim's Progress" may just be a developmental fantasy. Qabalah is another such model which itself is one example of the archetype of "The Way." We can alternatively examine archetypes from a non-hierarchal, pagan perspective. The real archetypal perspectives are manifold and open-ended, so make of them what you will.

We can also see archetypes existing as inter-related, separate-but-equal powers (as in Tarot). Then, the "stages-of-development fantasy" (dealing with an archetype at a time) fades into the background. Actually, their interaction in our lives is co-temporaneous and symphonic. Just noticing their presence in our lives adds a depth dimension and creates a relationship with them - a connection to inner resources and potential.

Both viewpoints illustrate a way of approaching the exploration of the psyche. Once we can embrace divergent points-of-view without conflict, we can use them both as tools. This prevents a one-sided dogmatism. We can learn to appreciate the various styles of awareness. The key concept is the sovereignty of each god within its domain. In this manner, by choosing to experience a broad range of consciousness states through identification, we gain tolerance for other viewpoints.

The developmental model is monotheistic--it emphasizes the ONE GOD seen through many forms. The polytheistic model recognizes the unique qualities of the various gods and goddesses. It is based on relatedness, not goal-oriented development. As a model of BEING not DOING, it provides another perspective than that of the over-achieving heroic ego and its manic quest for "more and better."

The world appears to us as we were conditioned to experience it. Archetypal influence acts like a lens, filtering our direct sensory experience and inner interpretations about the nature of reality. Different archetypes can cause us to alter viewpoints dramatically. Gods (as personified archetypes) affect our styles of consciousness, as well as our moods or states of consciousness. It is essential when one attempts individuation, to maintain awareness of the union of opposites within each person.

Each individual life has a dominant theme which emerges from the various potentials. Discovering our basic pattern we may live it consciously and intelligently, cooperating with the trend of this life pattern, rather than being dragged along unwillingly. Our outer fate is, then, transmuted into an inner experience and our true individuality begins to emerge.

This is an important step in the quest for the Self, individual wholeness, or well-being. It doesn't mean finding our personal mythology as much as plumbing the entire mythological level of our psyche. Another element of reality is when we (as humans) are immersed in the archetypal world. Here, psyche is the primary reality and extends beyond the human psyche. We are an inseparable part of that web-work of relationships whether we are consciously aware of it or not.

Practical Techniques - For Realizing the Self

Even with all this discussion on archetypes and imagination, you may still be at a loss as to how you may actually contact and recognize these internal forces. The answer is practice, and taking the time to notice. Two techniques are immediately accessible. One, from Jungian Psychology, is known as Active Imagination; the second, from the Hermetic Qabalah, is known as Pathworking. Both require a thorough understanding of the nature of imagination. Both culminate in a spontaneous internal dialogue with personified archetypes.

Exploration of the soul is possible through imagination--through consciousness journeys. In fact, soul or Psyche is Imagination. It is both a realm of experience and a human faculty. The realm of soul lies between and joins together those of matter and spirit. In other words, *the realm of Imagination lies between the physical world and perceptions and the spiritual level of conceptualization.*

We needn't go to sleep to experience this rich inner world; in fact, we frequently get glimpses of it in our daydreams. But, daydreams are something our ego makes up to serve its own desires--we make things up in daydreams to be the way we want them. Deeper levels of the imagination simply *happen to us*. The scenario doesn't serve the ego, but the higher Self. At this level, imagination is autonomous, and we simply immerse ourselves in that stream of consciousness.

Therapeutic process work provides a way and place for applying watchful or sustained attention to our inner imagery. A process helps us penetrate even deeper into the levels of the imagination or universal consciousness field. The imagination forms a middle ground where life and meaning merge, producing images.

Imagination is the realm of sacred psychology which approaches the gods through imagining and personifying, rather than through ritual, prayer, and sacrifice with a religious orientation. Imagination is a primary reality with a non-verbal, non-linear logic of its own. Archetypes function like the "strange attractors" of deterministic chaos, ordering the contents of the psyche. We can learn to orient ourselves to internal and external reality by noticing and responding to the images, sensations, and emotions we experience in imaginal encounters.

Comprehensive theories of the imagination distinguish three types of imaginative experience:
   1) everyday conscious imagining
   2) Jung's active imagination and other process work
   3) archetypal or visionary imagination

Therefore, active imagination gives us entree to the world of imagination. Once you are proficient at this technique, you might try the "visionary" mode. Both are experiential. They can be entered as dialogues of ego and Self, I and Not-I, or direct identification.

The imaginal world is the result of an overlapping of our emotional and higher mental faculties. In metaphysical terms, it consists partly of the Astral and Causal levels of experience. These terms are antiquated, implying a causal relationship. Archetypes are deterministic--unpredictable at any given moment, yet operating in distinguishable parameters. This is the characteristic of a chaotic system, one that is complex, dynamic, and subject to turbulence. The imaginal world reflects this chaotic, bizarre pattern. It is paradoxical, neither perceptual nor conceptual, but intermediate.

The three modes of interaction of the conscious and subconscious forces in imaginal encounters may be summarized as follows:

1). *Everyday Conscious Imaging* is where the ego is under the illusion that it is controlling the content of the vision. The ego feels proud of this "fantasy of control" over the imagination. But, the subconscious has a surprise in store for the ego and may respond, sooner or later, with a powerful eruption of images and emotions which the ego cannot contain.

At this point, the ego's image of itself fragments and the personality is profoundly disrupted. There may be images of dismemberment, apocalypse, or even ego death. The opposite driving power of the subconscious is now brought to the surface (into daily life) demanding some form of reconciliation. This occurs in all of our crises in life when we can no longer cope with our old methods of keeping it together.

2). *Active Imagination* is a means of addressing this problem to gain self-knowledge rather than being overwhelmed and impotent to face the challenge life is offering us. Our stunned ego can eventually develop a means of coping with these inner forces; in fact, it is an imperative necessity. When we actively engage the imagination, symbols of the Self appear spontaneously to reintegrate the fragmented personality (rebirth, resurrection).

Active imagination also involves an element of control of the direction the imaginal journey takes, but not for the benefit of the ego. It is to ensure the progressive unfolding of an imaginative sequence. Ego works with the tendencies of the psyche, seeking guidance from inner figures to achieve movement into a new situation or level of being. This results in an increased awareness of your internal processes.

Active imagination works through visualization and multi-sensory images (kinesthetic, visceral, audio, olfactory); sometimes the senses meld and appear in non-ordinary ways.

The practice of active imagination requires six steps:

Step 1: The preliminary phase requires focusing on your immediate life problems or aspirations to establish the intent or goal of the operation. If there is a problem or issue, it should be identified. The excursion into the imagination should have a well-defined purpose.

Step 2: Next, drop into a sort of reverie (natural trance) where you are physically and mentally relaxed. Assume a position where you are comfortable, but will not fall asleep. EMPTY THE MIND of the train of thought of the ego. If thoughts crop up, just watch them come and go, dismissing them if they deal with your outer life.

Step 3: This is the phase of letting go to your unconscious stream of images and letting that absorb your attention. (If you are Pathworking, visualize the corresponding Tarot Trump at this point and enter into its scenery). Focus on this image, but not enough to arrest the activity taking place. Don't make a frozen picture of it but, on the other hand, don't let it change too quickly. If this happens, you will find yourself looking at an inner movie instead of participating in a drama.

Step 4: Active imagination requires an ethical confrontation with the archetypal forces to be truly transforming. You must enter the inner drama with your true personality, not as you wish you were. Be the unique person you are in inner as well as outer life. Once the imaginal experience begins, the ego is compelled to participate. Take advantage of the opportunity to ask these forces just what they are seeking from you as a mortal being. See if the god-form has any gifts or treasures for you to take back into the day-world.

Step 5: The gifts of these forces take many forms, some of which are healing, physically and emotionally. The idea of this stage is to apply what you have learned in the encounter and make it practical. The god-form may have ordered or asked for certain behavior on the part of the ego. If this does not contradict cultural, moral, or ethical laws, you may experiment with these inner directions. In any event, the contact is established and you will know where and to whom to return if there is further need of "discussion."

Step 6: If you have had an intriguing inner journey and met the god-form in imagination by directing the unfolding of the fantasy, give it some form of expression in your external life. For example, write it down in your journal of inner events (or dream book), paint what you saw, sculpt it, dance it, or play the music you heard there.

Note of Caution

There is the chance of repressed unconscious forces breaking through into daily life, overwhelming the ego. If you feel emotionally unstable, seek a therapist to function as a guide on your inner journeys. There is a great deal of energy locked up, or stuck in past traumas, which need to be released. Active imagination is a means of facing up to, and dealing with, these shadowy problems.

Active imagination may bring unusual manifestations in its wake, including psychosomatic manifestations such as changes in blood pressure or heartbeat. These are caused by strong emotions and can be worked through by consciously relaxing oneself.

Alternatively, one might experience a strong sense of euphoria as the ego identifies with the archetypal forces during the event. There might be a reactionary let-down, but it won't last long.

Synchronistic events, or seemingly magical, meaningful coincidences, may appear. Don't let your judgment be blurred by excitement as this is a "normal" occurrence when working on the inner levels and provides additional insight on the processes at work.

Guideline for Practice:

1). Maintain a critical distinction between wish *fulfillment* and the experience of true imagination.

2). There is no rush to experience every god-form or Tarot Path via imagination. Take it slowly, learning and assimilating each new experience thoroughly before going further.

3). Insure your freedom from interruption during your imaginal excursion.

4). Establish a time limit; it is a good idea to have a trusted friend nearby to monitor you.

5). Record results in your journal (diary), including physical plane reactions and synchronicities.

6). Never do an active imagination which concerns living persons (includes especially intentional visualization of them in sexual fantasies). This is unethical, from the magician's point of view, as it is an encroachment on their *True Will*. (Chapter 8) It is an improper application of the technique.

7). Ground exercises in active imagination by applying the experiences gained in Pathworking to daily life.

8). Try to establish contact with your personal "inner guide" who will always offer protection if requested and allowed to do so.

Mythical Living:

Pathworking, using the Qabalistic diagram *The Tree of Life*, has much in common with active imagination. It consists in taking an imaginal journey to the "location" of an archetypal form. Once you can recognize that imagination is the realm of soul, you can acquire a method for exploring the soul through imagination. The paths of *The Tree of Life* function as metaphorical "inroads." Their correspondences produce an awareness of soul through their own system of metaphorical language.

One can also determine three major modes of Pathworking:

1). *Trance-like state* where the ego is overwhelmed (possibly through drug use) and incapacitated by the forces of the unconscious;

2). "*Active Pathworking*;" and

3). "*Passive*" Pathworking. The first form is a regression of consciousness and produces hallucinatory, not imaginal experiences.

Active Pathworking is analogous to active imagination. The major purpose of Pathworking is to produce a conscious contact with the archetypal powers connected with the particular path. There are active and passive forms of Pathworking, but do not let this terminology lead you astray. "Passive," in this sense, does not imply the ineffective attitude of type-1 experience. Both active and passive styles are desirable to develop. *Passive Pathworking* is analogous to visionary imagination.

Active Pathworking is an exercise of the creative imagination which is an excursion or consciousness journey into the astral plane through the faculty of clairvoyance. It is a combination of ego, will, and imagination. Pathworking produces an imagery state. It surpasses sensory information processing, but precedes conceptual lucidity. This is not a trance state where the images transform freely from one to another, but a disciplined artform, much like music, painting, or dance.

Clairvoyance means seeing the inner world with increasing clarity. This clarity comes through the ego's conscious participation. The main use of active Pathworking is for introspection. In Pathworking, the will forces the image to maintain certain parameters (determined by the Qabalistic correspondence system). The "will," in turn, is brought into direct non-verbal contact with the non-rational. In other words, the communication is generally visual rather than verbal.

Pathworking is a dynamic process which requires us to react to situations immediately through our feelings or instincts. It is similar to (but more profound than) some of the video games on the market today which reflect *The Quest*. The difference is, in Pathworking, the *Will* maintains a sense of responsibility for the ego's behavior on the inner planes. All one's faculties must be kept alert. Both cognition and emotional perception are involved. The ego's forceful elaboration helps to ensure the unfolding of a particular imaginative sequence.

An active Pathworking traces the routes described in Qabalah as the transition stages between spheres--moving from one state of consciousness to another by following a thread or path of imagery. A Pathworking begins in one sphere and culminates in the sphere immediately higher on *The Tree of Life*.

Any time two particular terminals are used, the traveler establishes a contact with both the "place" and the "entities" that are to be found inhabiting the psychological "area." With repetition, the imaginal reality of the place is confirmed through personal experience. You can evoke this experience from your own imagination, if you try, and become a regular visitor to these regions.

Always remember in Pathworking to return to your point of origin. This is one main reason the ego must be able to maintain concentration and follow-through. If you use a Tarot Trump as the gateway to your experience, be sure you pass through it on your way "out." You will visualize all you saw on your approach fleeting by on your "return." You ground your Pathworking by returning consciousness to its normal condition.

Visionary Imagination (or *Archetypal Imagination*) is analogous to passive Pathworking. *All images are archetypal in that they carry enfolded information about primal reality (holographic)*. This form of imaginal journey is termed passive since ego-consciousness is present, but that does not interfere with the unfolding of psychic imagery.

This *passive Pathworking* is actually more advanced because the traveler must employ his creativity or ability to synthesize information. The practitioner requires an ability to deal with the opening of the lower, as well as higher mind. We want to penetrate to super-celestial regions, not suffer an invasion from the primitive unconscious.

This form of Pathworking uses a doorway of some type to initiate the experience. This might again be a Tarot card, god-form visualization, or an I-Ching Hexagram (Exercise A), or even a last night's dream image. The difference is, that instead of following procedural instructions on where to go, and what to visualize, we allow the Pathworking itself to present the images.

This world we are describing is that revealed to us through the world's great artists, like Leonardo daVinci, Michelangelo, William Blake, etc. Regardless of when they lived, these men and women exemplify the Renaissance-type of spirit which lives close to world of myth and personified archetypal forces. These show on the canvas as demons, angels, gods and goddesses.

This passive Pathworking may be likened in some respects to what is termed "archetypal imagination" in avant-garde forms of Jungian Psychology. It is an authentic visionary mode of experience which produces keen insight through psychological perception.

If the main purpose of Pathworking is to contact the archetypal powers behind it, an examination of the meaning of "archetypal" becomes useful. Archetypal Theory has four general premises:

    1. Archetypes are located in the imaginal world of the Soul and were known from ancient times as gods and goddesses.

    2. Psychopathology (negative manifestations), which lead to human problems, is emphasized.

    3. Archetypes are extremely important to human behavior and seem to carry a quality of "unknowns" and holiness or divinity.

    4. The ego comes to realize it is only one psychological perspective and understands its relative lack of control over our psychic and physical organism.

Archetypal imagination transcends active imagination by offering a method whereby we can learn to redeem some dignity through our suffering. In archetypal psychology, pathologies (archetypal afflictions) are recognized as an essential component of the human soul.

Therefore, these psychologists explore the divine by insight into the light and dark aspects of the gods. Greek mythology is replete with many versions of divine images of darkness, death, and perversion, reflecting the world of mental illness. These divine forces are so powerful the ego cannot really "do" anything to them.

Like the Qabalah, archetypal psychology recognizes many varieties of consciousness which reflect the plurality and freedom of styles within the structure of myth. Since there are no procedural constraints in this passive Pathworking, what can we expect to experience through this awakened visionary mode? This is the realm of true inner plane contact with the deities revealed through folktales, classical myths, and in psychology through dreams.

To experience a luminously visionary imagination, we must become acquainted with the archetypes through personifying their potent forces. An archetypal topography, or psychic roadmap is of inestimable value here. QBL is a generic roadmap, of the psyche. It provides the possibility of interaction of an individual with the divine, immortal forms.

There is a long tradition throughout mankind's history which regards personifying as a necessary mode of comprehending the world and our personal existence. It is a way of ensiling psychic powers and getting to know them intimately. Personifying allows us to discriminate among, and love or cherish, these forces which make up our very being.

Personification is a path with heart since it allows us to imagine both through and beyond what our eyes see into the primordial dimension of celestial beings. Loving is a special way of "knowing" which arises from personification. The strong feelings aroused by subjective experiences of the soul speak volumes to the heart.

We can develop a passionate engagement with the mythic dimension, gaining access to our creative imagination. Through getting to know the gods within, we learn to see visions and hear voices. We may talk with them and they may talk with each other without us being at all insane.

We can speak directly to these archetypal forces within. When we do, the basic transformative formula is always the same. In terms of self-analysis there are three distinct steps:

1). *Identify the problem.* Name the neurotic pattern to loosen its grip on the identity and seek the help of inner spiritual guiding principles. This means we will have to suffer consciousness of our condition. No more "ignorance is bliss." We come to recognize our bad habits, and they seem to have amplified. Actually we are much as we have always been, but we have never turned our attention in this direction before. We may suffer a terrible, proud ego (Zeus), or a tendency to dishonesty with ourselves and others (Hermes), or an irresistible urge for an affair (Aphrodite).. But, our plight will no longer be unconscious once we have named it.

2). *Accept that suffering and find meaning in it.* Don't be a passive victim; face up to the shadow of outgrown behavior patterns and power-trips. Confront the negative forces of the psyche by mustering inner strength. Once you name a neurotic pattern, you claim it as a part of yourself; to deny this fact is to deny one's wholeness. When you consciously relate to its source, the "problem" is automatically transformed.

3). *Try to accept and manifest the potential strength of the inner self once it is called up.* In other words, once you have an imaginal contact with the archetype, try to contact its potential for positive transformation. Experience the more exalted qualities of the archetype as well as its instinctual, compulsive side. Don't give up because to passively withdraw means to stay stuck in the neurotic patterns.

Confront inner and outer crises with the reserves of strength made accessible through creative imagination.

Metaphorical Perception of the Experience:

Creative Mythology is another application of the gods within - personal my-thology. It is the result of combining creative imagination with a mythical per-spective on life. When we see through to the mythic patterns enacted in our lives on an on-going basis, we are living mythically as a lifestyle. Our personal history becomes a metaphorical analog of ancient, divine patterns, weaving an eternal tapestry.

Our personal mythic enactments can provide a focal point for our meditations concerning our own existence. When we get caught in the crises of our arche-typal complexes, we are again and again faced with the basic questions of life: *"Who am I; where do I come from; and where am I going?"* When we con-sciously seek an answer, we are looking for the meaning of existence. We seek to unfold our awareness of totality and we begin to see the gods everywhere.

Myth supports all the levels of our human civilization which include spiritual, social, and individual (or psychological). We seek a return to the mythic di-mension to find out how we personally relate to the cosmic order. In the mod-ern search for meaning, we are thrown back on our own resources. For a time, the social limits no longer apply since they don't provide an adequate model for our experiences.

During this period, we gain a vivid relationship to the symbols and dynamics of the subconscious and reestablish this vital connection. In this rebirth, or renewal, symbols take on the highest personal value. What seemed a life-less concept takes on depth and life. Development of our latent subconscious powers becomes possible.

Myth represents a paradoxical world with exquisite differentiation. For ex-ample, the Greeks had different specific names for the gods in their various facets. Thus Hermes could be simultaneously the god of writers, merchants, and magicians besides that of thieves and liars. In each of these aspects, he would have a different appellation to identify the specific aspect of Hermes in action. Most of the gods also have an infernal or chthonic aspect. It embodies their negative or shadowy nature.

We aren't to look at myths as prescriptions for living when we find we are caught in a particular one. They do not provide solutions to our personal problems if we can but read ahead a few pages. They won't tell us what step to take next, or right from wrong.

We obtain their value from participation in mythical consciousness, finding the gods as mythic metaphors living through our daily lives. We participate with them when we recognize their mythic enactments.

Mythical living provides us with a background which starts us imagining, penetrating deeper into ourselves, gaining in self-awareness. It is a mode of reflection. Myths do not show us the center of our selves; they reveal that there are several centers, all interrelated with one another in dynamic relationships.

Personification is also a key for mythical living. It is the mode of viewing archetypal processes from a psychological perspective which sees them as gods and goddesses. This method allows us to love the gods and focus our attention on them. Man has a symbiotic relationship with the gods. Their names give us the ability to call upon them.

This process of devotion takes place in the imaginal realm of the heart and has the power to transmute our outer fate into our inner destiny. It allows our true individuality to emerge. To achieve this, we must turn toward the archetypal realm and actively seek admittance.

See Workbook 1: Exercise D - Pantheon of Archetypal Gods in Daily Living

7

RESONANCE

KHWAN TRIGRAM

HISTORICAL CONTEXT – *Since the official scientific validation of brainwave entrainment back in 1959, research and brain studies into this new science had serious intent. It was Gerald Oster's* Auditory Beats in the Brain *(Scientific American, 1973) which greatly extended the range of research in biofeedback.*

Brainwave entrainment was a powerful cognitive and neurological research tool. More than 20% of The Seal Report *work was in and around these concepts, and how to integrate them into making a super soldier. With proper training, you could pass polygraphs and most interrogation techniques (used back then).*

The historic context was its use for mind control, and how to measure the autonomic nervous system. Certain altered states of consciousness could be used for a host of paranormal abilities. It allowed a kind of resonance in consciousness working with gut feelings.

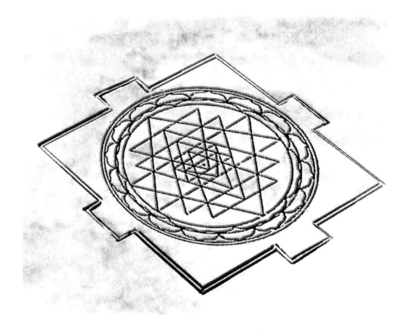

CROP CIRCLE

Western Oregon August 10, 1990

Chapter Seven

Frequency Studies
& Brain Entrainment

An ancient musician informed me, that there were some famous lutes that at-
tained not their full seasoning and best resonance till they were about fourscore
years old.

—ROBERT BOYLE [*1662*]

Theoretically, the practice of meditation is intended to withdraw the personal mind from its persistent preoccupation with external affairs. It can be seen as a form of training for the mind in switching from matter to psyche. There is a purpose: It is to prepare the personal nature so that it is able to reflect and express its relationship with the Universal Self.

Throughout history there have been a number of techniques used to achieve a meditative state. The most often used first step is a form of rhythmic breath-ing. If done correctly, a sequence of strong and unusual body reactions occur. These also will, eventually, trigger unusual psychological states via a type of resonance effect. A closer examination of these resonance-relationships yields information useful in improving the meditation.

Perhaps an example clarifies this: When a subject is totally relaxed and has achieved a deep meditative state, a slow, rhythmic sine wave pattern can be registered by a cardiograph-type sensing device. What is being measured is a standing wave in the aorta. There is a heart-aorta resonating oscillator which affects other parts of the body, including the brain.

Resonance occurs when the natural vibration frequency of a body is greatly amplified by vibrations at the same frequency from another body. Oscillators alter the environment in a periodic manner. When in a deep meditative state, the regular movement of the body indicates that a standing wave is set up in the vascular system, specifically in the aorta.

This standing wave affects several other resonate systems in the body, all of which are driven by this large signal.

The Concept of Soma

During Vedic, and pre-Vedic periods [*Satapatha Brahman* and *Taittireva Sanhita*], there were certain times of each month when the priests would meditate on specific symbols. The belief was that if one meditated in synchronization with the phases of the moon, it could be compared to riding on a swing.

A kick, at the right point, put more energy into the swing than at any other point. It was believed that meditation on certain symbols, at specific times related to these moon phases would add soma (internal energy) into the body more than at other times of the month. This produced optimal spiritual balance and growth.

Farmers and gardeners have known for centuries the profound differences in weather, plant growth, and seed-timing associated with lunar phases. Newer research shows the moon's effect on the EM-fields of the earth and their subsequent biological influences. Specific examples can be found in the lunar sex cycle of the female (cosmobiology) and, minus gender - insomnia and unstable mental states during a Full Moon.

Myth states that inspiration of the moon comes from the dark phases and from the soma drink which is brewed from the moon tree. It is not embodied in rational thought, but lies in the dark obscure movements, thoughts, and impulses of darkness. It manifests as an intoxicant, producing an enthusiasm which may even lead to madness.

Soma (internal energy) was considered a universal life power dispensed in great abundance during the waning moon. It could be absorbed directly by man in meditative states without having to ingest any plant at all. Certain plants were held particularly efficient in collecting and storing *soma*. When eaten, these plants that had the power to change consciousness were held sacred as embodiments of deities.

Psychologically, the ritual for absorbing soma is designed for relating oneself properly to the feminine principle. Then, one gains access to the eternal, immovable aspect of psyche, the reality of Self. When drinking in soma, the initiate becomes filled with the god. The inner voice of the daemon speaks, uncensored, and takes control for a time.

In Magick this is called *"assuming the god-form."* Through communion in the meditative process, an individual becomes acquainted with his own limits, depths, and ultimate reality. The highest incarnation of the female form of the Holy Spirit confers the deepest revelation.

There is a familiar passage from the Hermetic texts called *The Veil*. It states that the veil signified the Veil of the Universe or Robe of Isis. Crowley said this Veiled Isis *"is clothed only in the luminous veil of light. It is important for high initiation to regard Light not as the perfect manifestation of Eternal Spirit, but rather as the veil which hides that Spirit."*

These passages might be read as an exhortation to penetrate past the brightly-lit region of Tiphareth (solar consciousness). Lunar consciousness is a more diffuse awareness, an ability to discern in the dimly lit regions of the unconscious. That is why the Moon is associated with the *unknown* part of self.

True initiation implies breaking through the This Veil. This is the spiritual nature of man himself; to raise it means to transcend the limits of individuality and become consciously conscious of immortality. The Soul is, then, released from the constraints of time, space, and ego-orientation.

Turning psychological energy inward (by meditation) is a characteristically feminine process. This produces the psychic child which corresponds to Jung's concept of individuation. Its greatest value is attached to an activity of the creative imagination known as soul-making. Careful aesthetic elaboration of an event is its significance.

In *soul-making*, there is no separation between an event and its meaning. A sense of the sacred is, thereby, returned to daily activity. This inner marriage of masculine and feminine components gives birth to the inner child and release from the power of death. This child, the Self, is the fruit of psychic development.

In yogic practice, soma is also associated with the inner moon chakra, analogous to the pituitary and pineal glands. This inner moon is said to shower subtle secretions, or soma drops, which nourish the psycho-organism. These glands directly influence physiological processes. The pituitary regulates, among other functions, sex hormones, metabolism, and the growth and development of the individual.

Richard Wurtman, of M.I.T., states that stress activates the pineal gland. This, then, exerts an inhibitory influence on the body's stress mechanism (the hypothalmic-pituitary-adrenal axis). In view of the pineal gland's sedative effect on the Central Nervous System, *"the ancient mystics may have had something when they attributed effects of meditation to the pineal gland."*

Brainwave States

There are several types of brainwave states grouped into specific and distinct behaviors. Our brain consistently cycles through each of these brainwave states many times throughout the day and night. It is a completely natural biological occurrence in every human being.

Our brain does not operate in only one brainwave state at a time but, instead, pulses in all these brainwave states simultaneously with one of the states being dominant at any given time. The dominant state indicates our "state of mind" or level of consciousness. Each of these brainwave states occurs in a specific frequency band.

Beta - 13Hz to 40Hz - The Beta brainwave state is associated with a heightened state of alertness and focused concentration. When your mind is actively engaged in mental activities, the dominant brainwave state will be Beta. A person in active conversation, playing sports or making a presentation would be in a Beta state.

Alpha - 8 Hz to 12 Hz - Alpha brainwaves are slower in frequency than beta brainwaves and represent a state of relaxed mental awareness or reflection. Alpha brainwave states are typically associated with contemplation, visualization, problem solving and accessing deeper levels of creativity.

Theta - 4Hz to 8 Hz - Theta brainwaves are even slower in frequency and represent a state of deep relaxation and meditation, enhanced creativity, stress relief, light sleep and dreaming. Theta brainwave states have been used in meditation for centuries. Research has proven thirty minutes a day of Theta meditation can dramatically improve a person's overall health and well-being. Theta meditation has also been known to cause the need for less sleep.

Delta - 0Hz to 4Hz - Delta brainwaves are the slowest in frequency and represent a state of deep, dreamless sleep. Delta brainwave states have long been associated with healing. While Delta brainwave states usually only occur in deep sleep, it is possible to train yourself to remain awake while reaching the Delta state to experience even deeper levels of meditation and awareness.

Gamma - 40Hz or higher - Gamma brainwave states are the most rapid in frequency. They have received the least attention and research, although more attention is currently being paid to them than in years past. Research has indicated at moments when bursts of precognition or high-level information processing occur, your brainwaves briefly reach the Gamma state.

With the help of the brain driver audio technology, one can guide your brain into most of these brainwave states, naturally and effortlessly, simply by listening to an audio CD using stereo headphones. No special equipment is required. As long as you are using stereo headphones, you can listen via your stereo, a portable CD player, or even your computer's CD-ROM drive.

Binaural Beats

Binaural beats were originally discovered in 1839 by German experimenter, H. W. Dove. He discovered when signals of two different frequencies are presented separately, one to each ear, the brain detects the phase variation between the frequencies and tries to "reconcile" that difference.

In doing so, as the two frequencies mesh in and out of phase, the brain creates its own third "phantom" signal - a *binaural* beat - equal to the difference between those two frequencies.

For example, if a frequency of 100 Hz is presented to the left ear and a frequency of 105 Hz is presented to the right ear, the brain "hears" a third frequency pulsing at 5 Hz, the exact difference between the two frequencies.

Research has proven that introducing a binaural beat will cause the brain to begin resonating in tune with the frequency of that beat. This is called the *frequency following response* and was thoroughly researched and tested in 1973 by biophysicist Gerald Oster at Mount Sinai Hospital in New York City.

Oster's research on binaural beats and the frequency following response was published in Scientific American (Scientific American - May 1963 - Vol. 208 - No. 5) and paved the way for further development in the area of auditory stimulation to enhance brain functioning. Since that time, binaural beat technology has been endorsed by scores of doctors and scientists around the world.

Oster's works included the concept of Moiré Patterns. Anyone who has traveled over a bridge in an automobile has seen interesting patterns that result from the superposition of vertical fencing and other repetitious ironwork. The interesting figures observed are called Moiré patterns.

Fascinating patterns can be obtained by overlaying appropriate grids. A simple example is given below. Similar grids that have radial lines of variable pitch and line width, when overlaid, can give the pattern shown. This is part of "what happens" when two frequencies are beat together in the brain.

 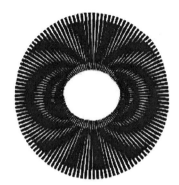

Frequency Following Response

By introducing a binaural beat via stereo headphones, we can guide our brain into very specific brainwave frequencies via the Frequency Following Response.

For example, by listening to a binaural beat pulsing at a frequency of 5 Hz, a low Theta frequency, we can trigger our brain to resonate at that same 5 Hz frequency, automatically inducing brainwaves in the Theta range. By listening to a binaural beat pulsing at a frequency of 10Hz, an Alpha frequency, we can effortlessly guide our mind into the Alpha range.

When our brain begins to resonate with the binaural beat, or "follow" along with the beat, it is called the *Frequency Following Response.*

While the scientific effects of binaural beats on the brain were not formally studied until the past century, various cultures have been inducing the frequency following response through more primitive means for thousands of years.

By introducing a harmonically layered combination of frequencies and binaural beats to your brain via the audio technology (like Holosync), you can effortlessly induce amazingly powerful states of focused concentration or deep relaxing meditation while stimulating various parts of your brain to work together in synchronization.

Whole Brain Synchronization

When both hemispheres of the brain begin to resonate to the binaural beat in synchronization, this is called "whole brain synchronization". This is also sometimes referred to as "whole brain functioning" or "hemispheric synchronization" (Monroe Institute's Hemisync).

Whole brain synchronization occurs when the various parts of our brain begin to work together, resonating at the same frequencies and causing neural pathways to fire more rapidly.

The left and right sides of our brain begin to work in concert with each other. Electrical activity and energy patterns in our brain become more widespread throughout the brain instead of remaining confined to certain areas. Our brain reaches extraordinary levels of consciousness not normally attainable without years of practice.

Research has indicated this type of "whole *brain synchronization*" is present in the brain at times, of intense creativity, clarity and inspiration. EEG patterns recorded from various test groups comprised of extremely successful individuals, also displayed an extraordinarily high level of "whole brain synchronization".

By listening to the Theta range forms, we can train your brain to function at this high level of synchronization, opening up the way for positive and beneficial effects. From the moment you first listen to these various audio technologies, our brain will begin the process of reorganizing itself for higher thinking and enhanced levels of consciousness.

Neural Development in the Brain

While using these various audio technologies, electrical activity and energy patterns in our brain become more widespread throughout the brain instead of remaining confined to certain areas.

When this type of stimulation to the brain occurs, our brain begins to create new neural pathways. The neural stimulation encourages new dendritic growth within the brain. New dendritic growth allows for faster and smoother neural communication in the brain and, also, provides more "processing power" in the brain.

The dendrites are the many branching fibers extending from the neuron/cell body. These fibers increase the surface area available for receiving incoming information. The more dendrites the brain has at its disposal, the more quickly and smoothly it can process information.

Dendritic growth is a process that occurs throughout our lifetime. Whenever we learn something new, such as learning to play the piano, new dendrite growth occurs as a result of stimulating the mind in a new and different way. At the same time, old dendrite connections can become inactive and dissipate. (The shortening of dendritic branches and the reduction of the number of branches are associated with senility in the elderly).

One of the goals in using audio technology is to stimulate dendritic growth to occur on an ongoing basis to provide an ideal situation for the brain. This allows the brain to operate at its maximum possible potential rather than only using a portion of its potential. The can, then, establish dendrite growth for long-term benefits, including counteracting the debilitating effects of aging.

There are also some hormonal drugs, like *Diapid* (vasopressin), which can enhance dendritic growth. Vasopresin is an anterior pituitary hormone that is taken by nasal injection. This hormone begins growing dendrites within seconds and is often used to help some forms of Alzheimer's disease.

Through this type of neural development and whole brain synchronization, the brain eventually learns to achieve more powerful states on its own, so that, in time, these states may be achieved at will.

Harmonically Layered Frequencies

Most companies offering binaural audio recordings stop with one frequency. This introduces only one binaural beat which may, gradually, raise or lower your brainwaves into a specific frequency over a period of time. This is usually in anywhere from 10 to 60 minutes.

What is wrong with only one binaural frequency is that the brain typically operates not in only one frequency but in all brainwave frequencies simulta-neously, with one frequency, typically being the dominant one at any given time. At any moment of the day and night, various brainwaves in the brain are pulsing in delta, theta, alpha, beta, and even gamma frequency ranges, all at the same time.

The brain has its own individual brainwave patterns, incorporating a combina-tion of all the frequencies pulsing in it. Just like fingerprints or vocal patterns, brainwave patterns are unique. This discovery has led to brain fingerprint-ing technology, now considered more than 10x more accurate than standard polygraph protocols.

Harmonically layering binaural frequencies will create actual patterns, not just single frequencies. If binaural frequencies are combined in a way that replicates the brain's natural way of functioning, this will evoke the most pow-erful responses on all levels.

Most current protocols also use a form of harmonic layering with a foundation in the principles of music science. The binaural frequencies are usually placed beneath the sounds of natural rain and are embedded below the audible lev-el. They are, therefore, not heard out loud in the same manner music would be heard. The brain still responds more effectively to binaural frequencies that are blended together in a harmonically pleasing way that is soothing to the ear and mind.

This reduces the stress of expectation on the brain and enhances the effectiveness of the audio technology and allows our brain to resonate smoothly and comfortably with the binaural beats. When most companies refer to a "harmonic matrix," they are referring to a very simple and unsophisticated method of layering binaural frequencies. That type of "harmonic matrix" is quite easy to reproduce and is not at all like the more complex and sophisticated harmonic layering process used in more advanced audio technology.

The more simple forms of harmonic matrix are typically any number of "layers" or pairs of frequencies. Rather than a single pair of frequencies used to trigger a binaural beat, they use multiple pairs of frequencies.

For example, one of the soundtracks might contain one pair of frequencies at 200Hz and 205Hz (to trigger a 5Hz binaural beat), another pair at 230Hz and 235Hz (for the same 5Hz binaural beat), another pair at 270Hz and 275Hz (again, for the same 5Hz binaural beat), and so forth, all playing simultaneously within the same track.

Occasionally, the amplitude of one pair of frequencies might vary to make it stronger than the others. That process of using various pairs of frequencies is what is referred to as a "*harmonic matrix*". There is, of course, nothing musically *harmonic* about their process and the word "harmonic" is simply used - or misused, in this case - because multiple layers of frequencies are being used.

The newer and more sophisticated processes do not involve selecting just a few random pairs of frequencies and layering them. Instead, they arrange the frequencies more precisely, subtly shifting them throughout the entire course of each track. This is to maintain specific harmonic combinations as the track progresses.

Binaural frequencies are placed beneath the sounds of natural rain, and are embedded at a very low, audible level. They are not heard out loud in the same manner music would be heard. The brain, however, still responds more effectively to binaural frequencies that are blended together in a harmonically pleasing way that is soothing to the ear and mind.

This enhances the effectiveness of the audio technology, allows our brain to resonate smoothly and comfortably with the binaural beat, improves the process of whole brain synchronization, and enhances the overall experience by actively engaging many areas of the brain rather than a select few areas.

By introducing these harmonically layered binaural frequencies, one can effortlessly trigger whole brain synchronization, enhancing communication between various parts of the brain and stimulating neural pathways in the brain to fire at increased rates.

From the droning chant of Tibetan monks to the rhythmic beat of a Native American drum, sound has played an important role in healing and spiritual practice throughout history. Primitive cultures were aware of the powerful and beneficial effects of binaural beats on the brain centuries before modern science recognized those same effects.

Research conducted by Melinda Maxfield, Ph.D., demonstrates how the drumbeats found in the rituals of various cultures beat at a steady rate of 4.5 beats per second, inducing a trance-like state in listeners. This trance-like state is a result of the brain's shift into a 4.5-beats-per-second brainwave pattern, a low theta brainwave state.

Using repetitive beats or chanting, Native American shamans, Hindu healers, Tibetan monks, Sufi dervishes, and practiced Yogis have been able to induce an entire range of brainwave states for healing and the attainment of higher levels of consciousness. In India, there exist songs and mantras created specifically for use in curing illness and disease, practiced by Babaji—Hindu healers—to heal even such medical problems as arthritis and smallpox.

Everywhere we turn, in every culture throughout history, binaural beats have been a powerful tool in the healing process, as well as a guide in spiritual ceremony and ritual.

Brainwave Entrainment

Brainwave entrainment was first identified in 1934, although its effects had been noted as early as Ptolemy. Not long after the discovery of the Alpha brainwave by Hans Berger in 1929, researchers found that the strength of the wave could be "driven" beyond its natural frequency using flickering lights.

In 1942, Dempsey and Morison discovered that repetitive tactile stimulation could also produce entrainment and, in 1959, Dr. Chatrian observed auditory entrainment in response to clicks at a frequency of 15 per second. This is called *"photic driving"* which is another word for brainwave entrainment using *photic* (light) stimulation.

By the 1960's entrainment started to become a tool rather than a phenomenon of the brain. Anesthesiologist M. S. Sadove, MD, used *photic* stimulation to reduce the amount of anesthesia needed for surgery. Bernard Margolis published an article on brainwave entrainment used during dental procedures noting less anesthesia required, less gagging, less bleeding and a general reduction in anxiety.

In a 1973 issue of Scientific American, Dr. Gerald Oster examined how combining two pure tones resulted in a rhythmic beat which he called Binaural and Monaural beats. In comparing binaural beats against monaural beats, Oster noted that monaural beats were shown to elicit extremely strong cortical responses, the electrical activity responsible for entrainment.

He concluded that while Binaural beats produced very little neural response (because the depth of a Binaural beat is only 3db or 1/10 the volume of a whisper), they could be useful in diagnosing certain neurological disorders.

The 1980's studies continued with Dr. Norm Shealy and Dr. Glen Solomon, researching entrainment for headache relief, Serotonin and HGH release, and general relaxation. Michael Hutchison wrote his landmark book *MegaBrain* in 1981, outlining the many possible uses of entrainment from meditation to super-learning.

In 1980, Tsuyoshi Inouye and associates, at the Department of Neuropsychiatry at Osaka University Medical School in Japan found that *Photic* stimulation produced "cerebral synchronization". Dr. Norman Shealy later confirmed the effect, finding that *photic* stimulation produced synchronization in more than 5,000 patients.

In 1984, Dr. Brockopp analyzed audio-visual brain stimulation and, in particular, hemispheric synchronization during EEG monitoring. He said, "*By inducing hemispheric coherence the machine can contribute to improved intellectual functioning of the brain.*" Arturo Manns published a study which indicated the amazingly strong entrainment value of Isochoric Tones as opposed to Monaural or Binaural beats. This was later confirmed by others such as David Siever.

Studies continued into the 90's with researchers such as Dr. Russell, Dr. Carter and others who explored the vast potential of using entrainment with ADD and learning disorders. Research has also been conducted into PMS, Chronic Fatigue, Chronic Pain, Depression, Hypertension and a number of other disorders.

Steady research continues today with the work of Dr. Thomas Budzynski, David Siever, psychologist Michael Joyce and many others. The results of entrainment have been so promising that many modern clinical EEG units now come with entrainment devices.

With over 70 years of solid research behind brainwave entrainment, why hasn't it become better known? Our culture is very much dependent on drugs and in comparison to the pharmaceutical giants, there is not a lot of money to be made in entrainment. It is inexpensive, easy to use at home and can be a viable solution to a huge variety of problems.

Brain Drivers

Brain driver technology uses harmonically layered frequencies to create binaural beats, inducing specific brainwave states and patterns when listened to via stereo headphones. These brainwave states are conducive to higher consciousness, profoundly deep meditation, enhanced clarity and concentration, and improved cognitive functioning.

They are now available for a multitude of uses. I began my use with them in an attempt to create a "meditative brain" associated with enlightenment. Basically, a person who has meditated for more than 30 years has a brain structured quite differently than normal brains. The question is, how anyone can get to these states quickly.

Like most *"short-cuts,"* there are layers in the learning coefficients. Using brain drivers can help create the brain-state of 30 years of meditation in less than three years. The down side is that these learned responses are not as well-grounded as those who do it for years. Like biofeedback, reinforcement is usually required every several years (for fine-tuning).

Stereo headphones or earphones are needed in order for the technology to have an effect. This is necessary for brain entrainment. They should have a frequency range of 20Hz–18,000Hz (or better). Most inexpensive headphones or earphones (under $15/pair) can reproduce this range of response.

Most brain driver products can be played with a CD's through a stereo, a portable CD player, or through your computer's CD-ROM drive. They all require that you are listening through stereo headphones.

It is not recommend to convert the CD tracks to MP3 files because of the potential degrading of audio quality. If the low-range frequencies are clipped during the conversion process, the effectiveness of the binaural audio could potentially be reduced.

While the Gateway, CenterPointe, and Brain Sync programs use binaural beats to induce specific brainwave states, adding virtual audio technology is superior.

Listening should be limited to no more than one hour per day. Listening for more than the recommended time could potentially cause the listener to feel overwhelmed. Also, brain drivers should not be used by anyone with a history of seizures or epilepsy and should not be used while driving or operating machinery.

They should not be used while performing tasks, or doing other things, because the deep, meditative effect will be diminished. It is recommended to use them while sitting in a comfortable chair with eyes closed. They may also be used while sitting on the floor in a more traditional meditation posture.

Use brain drivers, while awake, for relaxation or incredibly deep meditation and exploration of consciousness. Or, we can use them while drifting off to sleep at night, for dream exploration or for simply a more refreshing night's sleep. The long-term benefits of using brain drivers become more evident if used while one is awake and relaxing.

The natural tendency, when initially using brain drivers, is to fall asleep even if sitting upright in a comfortable chair or on the floor. This is a result of the audio technology taking your mind and body into a profoundly deep state of relaxation. Over time, you will begin to reach a point where you are able to remain awake throughout the session (if you choose).

Stray thoughts won't interfere at all with the use of brain drivers. Often, the thoughts experienced while listening are the result of our mind trying to work through and resolve mental and emotional issues, similar to the process our mind goes through nightly while dreaming. Letting the mind wander, while listening is sometimes the best approach to allow it to "find its way" to the solution it is searching for.

At times, you may find your thoughts overflowing with creative ideas during he listening session. These are all completely normal and healthy occurrences.

The sounds of rain are used to mask the sound of the binaural tones and to provide the most pleasant listening experience possible. In addition, it has been proven that masking the binaural tones with a form of white noise, such as rain, enhances the effectiveness of the tones.

The tones used to create the binaural beats are set at a level just below the sound of the rain. Many people do not hear the tones, but on occasion you might hear the slightest vibration or a very soft sound. For best results, you should not increase the volume on your CD player.

Enlightenment and the Brain

The experience of God has been produced in the laboratories of Laurentian University's Neurosciences program (Ottawa) and, for almost 30 years, been the study of Dr. Michael A. Persinger. His conclusion is that the *'God-experience"* reflects specific neural activity. This is quite a radical notion for the western world.

Eastern philosophy, however, places its crucial emphasis on enlightenment. The theories and hypotheses used to explain the experience of God should also be able to account for enlightenment. If not, then they cannot be the platform for a synthesis of science and spirituality.

The medieval concepts of consciousness were always *goal-oriented*. In western thought, it was to prevent *'sinful'* thoughts and feelings and to unite as closely to God as possible. In eastern philosophy of mystic traditions (not religions), the purpose was to help conquer anger, greed, sadness, ignorance, and to seek true enlightenment.

The one concept that all of these traditions agree upon is that to reach enlightenment is to end a discomfort intrinsic to being alive. Although it is possible to arrive there, what the various teachings seem to present as single state of consciousness is actually a whole range of states.

States of consciousness are now seen as diverse patterns of brain activity and all brain activity takes place within certain thresholds. The enlightened states may only be available to a few people with unique neural profiles; people with especially high or low thresholds in crucial brain parts.

For those of us who are seeking enlightenment, the crucial question is how high or low are these thresholds? If it's too difficult, normal brains might not be able to manage it. Those of us who are not prone to altered states of consciousness do not get the sense that our fulfillment lies in developing our consciousness.

For many, the peak moments of our lives, the ones we are most likely to try to achieve again, will lie within the range of normal states of consciousness. If we define a healthy mind as one that's always changing, then enlightenment becomes a coping mechanism for adjusting to the sensation of bliss. That leaves one to wonder if *"enlightened"* is all that healthy.

Trying to become enlightenment is not always the best way to enjoy consciousness. It can be likened to a carpenter who spends so much time sharpening his tools and then never getting any actual woodworking done. Our sense of self is said to change when a person becomes enlightened.

When this happens, we no longer identify ourselves with the 'old', nor do we take identity from it. No matter what else we may be, we are now *"another person"*. This is how the mind's-eye works (*visual imaging*) as a self-serving support system. This is all part of the concept of becoming enlightened.

The *Amygdala* and *Hippocampus*

The human sense of self is maintained in the limbic system which exists on both sides of the brain. A structure on the one side that feels good (when it's busy) is complimented by feeling bad on the opposite side. For most of us, this emotional structure (*amygdala*) feels good on the left side of the brain and bad on the right side.

For most of us, a cognitive, thinking structure called the *hippocampus* feels better on the right side and worse on the left. These two brain-parts are next to each other (inter-grown) and a normal brain has a positive and a negative emotional response on each side. A few, however, have *left-handed* limbic parts.

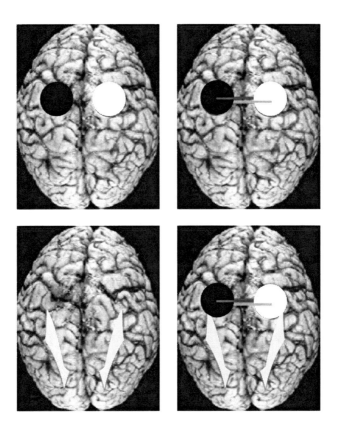

The Amygdala – our Emotional Structure. The left is specialized for positive emotions, while the right for negative emotions.

For the left-handed, the positive amygdala will be inter-grown with the positive hippocampus. Communication between the two will be much easier than in a normal brain. The other side of the brain will have strong communication between the negative hippocampus and the negative amygdala. These individuals tend to find themselves very emotionally sensitive.

When we stop to recall that most spiritual practices exclude negative thoughts and emotions, it seems possible that long-term practice might eventually stop their occurrence. More likely, a threshold might be passed that will leave positive emotions with lower thresholds than negative ones, and positive expectations for ongoing events becomes easier than the opposite.

> *This would suggest that meditation works by starving negativity rather than feeding virtue.*

If we accept that meditation is conducive to enlightenment, and that the moments when meditation appears in daily life are moments when negative states are wholly absent, then we get a new definition of enlightenment. It includes the complete absence of all unpleasant subjective states.

This is why training the mind (meditation) takes such unrelenting efforts. Fear, for example, is a powerful adaptive ally. Each thing that enters our perception is 'scanned' to see if it is a threat or not. Becoming enlightened would mean not doing this any longer. To stop *scanning for danger* would mean actually changing the matrices of neurons that support the human *sense of self* (as the higher mind).

Gradual enlightenment is easily explained in terms of more ordinary neural mechanisms. The consistent practice conditions the individual to suppress negativity so that more positive (and adaptive) emotional and cognitive responses can appear. Over time, changes on the smallest levels of brain activity alter the sense of self that relies on our thoughts and feelings.

Our Sense of Self:

Following Occam's razor, there are some simple rules about our sense *of self*. One is that our *sense of self* is partly made up of language. Although it's different for each person, we maintain a constant stream of inner dialog, talking to ourselves. We rehearse conversations before we have them, and when we lose an argument, we then spend time thinking of what we should have said.

The second rule is the *sense of self* may be aspects of a hallucination. The brain parts that support it are also the ones behind these hallucinations. In looking for the human self, science is coming up empty-handed. Cognitive science understands quite a bit about the modalities in which it operates, but not much about what holds them together.

The answer I suggest is that there is a sense that uses all the neural substrates of the other senses as it is organs and that has no 'percept'. Instead, it only hallucinates. And it has only one hallucination, the self. Or, more precisely, we actually have two of selves, one on each side of the brain.

The one on the left (where the language centers are) is the most active, so our experience of ourselves is shaped by words. It is our own inner dialog and the words we hear from others. The one on the right, the silent 'self', is constantly overwhelmed by the verbal 'self'. It remains subordinate.

Very few models of brain activity can encompass really sudden shifts in states of consciousness. While a seizure might be invoked to explain the suddenness of the event, the moment of enlightenment is not a recurring event the way seizures are. In the classical descriptions, enlightenment forever alters the *sense of self.*

If we think that enlightenment may not happen in this lifetime, then forget about the maximum potentials for our states of consciousness. A more direct approach would be to focus instead on our most immediate potential.

We really can't say that there is anything wrong with our life because we are not enlightened. Something might be wrong, but it is not being enlightened. More likely, it's too much anger, sadness, loneliness, sexual frustration, fear, or patterns (self destructive) we keep repeating. If our life was totally comfortable, why would we bother with spirituality?

> *It might be more productive to focus on what you want to get rid of in doing spiritual practice, instead of what you want to attain.*

So, why meditate? Because, meditation increases our sensitivity to our own anger, fear, or sadness. In meditation, we learn to be aware. As that happens, we become aware of our own emotions and feelings along with everything else in our experience, right as they happen. Most will find that we all are in some sort of discomfort most of the time, and that all of it comes from within.

As we become more aware, we see that each negative thing we create for ourselves is a process. It starts off with hearing somebody say something we don't like. We then have an emotional response. Our body gets tense. Our thoughts sprint into looking for a response. It is a whole process, not just one event.

The more aware we are, the sooner we notice that it is happening. If we notice it soon enough, we can re-route things. Response to our own negativity is a way to re-routing the brain's activity away from the amygdala. One of the functions of the hippocampus is monitoring inner states.

Just stopping to look at what is actually happening during a moment of negativity can change its course. If we do it frequently enough, we may find that completing our negative patterns does not become a habit. The brain parts that support negativity become less active when negative patterns cannot go anywhere, so the sense of self also changes.

A species that is really improving its ability to live isn't trying to arrive at a 'perfect' form.

The Schumann's Resonances

Paul F.J. New indicates the presence of a major resonate cavity oscillator located between the heart and the bifurcation where the aorta divides itself. When the timing of the pressure pulses traveling down the aorta coincide (in phase) with the reflected pressure pulse, a standing wave is achieved.

When this frequency approaches 7Hz, a progressively amplified wave form is created by resonance, resulting in a large oscillation affecting every other circuit in the body tuned to this frequency.

The Schumann resonances (SR) are a set of spectrum peaks in the extremely low frequency (ELF) portion of the Earth's electromagnetic field spectrum. Schumann resonances are global electromagnetic resonances excited by lightning discharges in the cavity formed by the Earth's surface and the ionosphere.

There is a resonance relationship to this frequency with standing waves on the Earth's crust. If we assume that the spherical crust of the Earth represents a condenser, then the frequency of resonance can be calculated on the basis of the equation:

$$f_n = \frac{c}{2\pi a} \sqrt{n(n+1)}$$

The letter c stands for the velocity of propagation of electromagnetic waves, the a = radius of the Earth, and letter n determines the harmonic mode, with the primary frequency at 7.83Hz.

Thus, a harmonic frequency corresponding to the pulsation of the electrical charge of the Earth is present in the heart/aorta.

The brain may be considered as a piezoelectric gel converting physical vibrations into electrical ones. Although the body movement from this heart/aorta resonance is relatively small, 0.003-0.009 mm, the head is a dense and tight structure. By moving up and down, the skull accelerates the brain with mild impacts.

These acoustical plane waves are reflected from the cranial vault and are focused upon the third and lateral ventricles. A hierarchy of frequencies couples this 7Hz body movement to the higher frequencies in the ventricles.

That which is that bright within the heart; in that this man resides, innate with mind transcending death, with brilliance innate.

TAITTIRIYA UPANISHAD

Bio-Cybernetics

In the book Biomedical Engineering Systems, Chapter 7, is a major work entitled "*Toward A View of Man*" by Manfred Clynes. Clynes is a medical doctor working at the Research Center in Rockman State Hospital, Orangeburg, New York. This work is now considered a breakthrough in the fields of psychology and medicine, known today as the field of psychobiology (bio-cybernetics).

Clynes took a number of volunteers and shaved their heads, placing a series of electrodes in rosette patterns on various regions of the brain. These included the temporal and frontal lobe section and occipital region. In this way, not only were the brain frequencies monitored, but directional shifts in these frequencies could also be determined by the geometry of the electrodes on the skull.

The original purpose of Clynes' work was to find out how precision and order exist in brain processes; to discover what is inherently programmed in man and how he might make use of the inherent programs.

These individuals were given a number of images (form) and colors to concentrate on while their brain was monitored by computers. Recording from opposite pairs of electrodes simultaneously, Clynes obtained views of the electrical activity from different angles: mathematically, a spatial differentiation of the electric vector.

What was happening literally was a mapping of consciousness. A number of very important observations were made:

1. Certain qualities and relationships were of great importance to the computer than such quantitative factors like intensity. This meant that the brain's systems of identification were based on differences, rather than intensity of the signal.

2. Thin lines were found to produce characteristic evoked potentials irrespective of size. The form itself is transduced into another form in the brain space time which can be measured. There is a one-to-one correspondence between the visual form of the stimulus, the response form in the brain, and the perception.

> *This is, perhaps, the first physical description of the field of an archetype. It is a geometrical structuring and has uniqueness.*

3. The process of inhibition is as important for transducing the external world as is excitation. Concentrating on specific lines of geometry does not constitute the changing stimulus, but their steady presence systematically and radically alters the response to another changing stimulus.

4. Changes in intensity of a single color produce very simple response shape. Light and darkness (as opposites) show no evidence of being different values of the same variable. Rather, they seem to be the result of stimulating and also, of inhibiting different receptors. This, the evoked potentials to light and darkness, in no way may be said to be positive and negative, respectively. White, for example, appears in this view as the result of mutual inhibition of color.

5. These experiments clearly imply an *inherent* form of organization and not a random learning of nerve nets. It is possible to mentally recognize and perceive the stimulus within the first portion of the invoked potential. Portions responding (in the brain) which occur later than 0.3 sec. are seen as systematic processes or tuned circuits to those responses to specific in-coming stimulus. This is a form of resonance in the brain to specific geometry. This could also lead to the formation of memory.

6. Every perception has a unique counterpart as a space-time code form in the brain. These space-time shapes are evidence of relationships between the external world and its representation in the brain. They act like keys to "unlock" specific parts of our brain, often being observed below psychological threshold levels (subliminal).

Clynes literally mapped fields in the human brain. A computer was able to identify and reproduce those geometrical figures from what that human was concentrating on, either as a geometric form or color. The individual did not even have to look at the pattern but simply concentrated "in his mind's eye." A standing wave means that the wave is not changed, but is holding itself steady in one certain geometrical thought.

If quantum mechanical properties of matter are actually the conscious property of matter, then one would predict that all phenomena, where quantum wave explanations are important, could be interpreted better in terms of consciousness.

The Geometry of Archetypes

Our planet is surrounded by a layer of electrically charged particles called the ionosphere. The lower layer of the ionosphere starts about 80km from the Earth. This charged layer is known to reflect radio waves.

Since this is a highly charged layer, the ionosphere forms a so-called capacitor with the Earth. This means that there is a difference in electrical potential between the two, the Earth being negatively charged and the ionosphere being positively charged. This potential varies somewhat, but is around 200 volts/m.

This is a fundamental type of electrical generator. The solar winds, interacting with the upper atmosphere rotation, act as a collector and brushes of a generator. The lower atmosphere can be seen as a storage battery for this gradient potential.

This electrostatic field around the Earth can be viewed as a stiff jelly. When our bodies move and vibrate, these movements are transmitted to the environment. These fields not only impinge on our body, but they also affect the charges inside our body. When we are standing on the ground, under normal conditions, we are grounded.

Our body, then, acts as a sink for the electrostatic field and we actually distort the force lines somewhat. Our body also has its own electrostatic field around itself. These field-lines are the result of the various biochemical reactions in the body. This resultant bio-field couples us to the electric field of the planet.

A "tuned system" consists of at least two oscillators of identical resonance frequencies. If one of the oscillators starts emitting, the other will be activated by the signal very shortly. Because the coupling is ideal, they will respond to the tiniest signals and begin to resonate.

In 1957, W.O. Schumann calculated the Earth-ionosphere cavity resonance frequencies. His works were updated over the years and the figure now used is at 7.83Hz. As indicated previously, the micro motion of the body is about 6.8 to 7.5Hz.

It is obvious that when we are in deep meditation, it is possible for the human being and the planet system to start resonating. There is a transfer of energy. It is no coincidence that this frequency is in the theta region of brainwaves, the state of maximum regeneration.

Information is embodied in a field rather than just being a field. A field is, thus, an abstract quantity of information; relationships between this point and that point in the universe. Astral temples are set up to evoke a certain correspondence effect, like a resonance. These temples are like a physical matrix, one with specific geometrical form and color.

The visualization, in turn, sets up a particular EM resonance in the brain. The reverberation pattern is most explicit. Clarity is all important. Distortion mini-mizes the resonance effect and reduces any amplification to connecting other "tuned" oscillators in the body.

Techniques of extending this harmonious resonance have been known for thousands of years. These are the different meditative techniques. Most slow down the metabolic rate of the body so that much less oxygen is required to keep the body going.

As we becomes proficient in meditation, our breathing becomes so gentle as not to disturb the resonate state of the aorta. An automatic process develops in which the lungs and the diaphragm regulate the heart-aorta system so as to keep them well-tuned. This helps extend the resonant behavior even with shallow breathing.

Resonance Effects in Meditation

The following points can now be made regarding the resonant effects available through meditation:

1. There is a heart/aorta resonance which links up with a number of other critical oscillators including several in the brain. It starts at the heart.

2. Specific geometries or geometrical mandalas (form and color) create resonance effects in the brain. The pattern is repeated in the brain.

3. Specific geometrical systems can be used as "keys" to access those specific archetypes. Access occurs to the psyche.

4. This linking of resonant cavity oscillators can be seen to form a common thread going from Hadit (DNA-RNA helix) to Nuit (galactic hydrogen-helium field).

5. By "tuning" our meditation, it is possible to amplify, and have access to, the other resonant systems, in and out of the body.

The human organism has usually been regarded as a complex arrangement of chemical elements and compounds. The quantity and structure of these variables are our reference points for states of health. This is the area of biochemistry and biochemical analysis.

An equally valid approach is to regard the human organism as an aggregation of electromagnetic fields which are constantly interacting and changing as are their biological equivalents. It has been shown that the human system is an emitter of electromagnetic radiations. All biological processes are a function of electromagnetic field interactions. EM fields are the connecting link between the world of form and resonant patterns.

The patterns are arbitrary forms which are non-physical. Archetypal forms are based on inherent characteristics and correspondences. This provides a basis for what we would call resonant phenomena in archetypal systems. EM fields embody or store gestalts, patterns of information.

*An archetype may then be seen as a specific geometrical system of stand-
ing waves occurring in the brain as a space-time shape (key).*

In living organisms, opposites receive their structure of symmetry from particular combinations of spatial and temporal aspects. Like reins on a horse, each
of the opposites of the psychological pair has its own place. This geometric
property makes them capable of being opposites. The activity of each arm
determines the quantity; the spatial identity of the rein determines the quality. There is no monotonic (or linear) transition from one to the other passing
through zero.

A human being, immersed in the galactic hydrogen-helium field, may also utilize the pulsing feedback between man and the galaxy to build up the resonance effects, much like we would tune a radio. These primary frequencies
are multiples of the base frequency 7.83 Hz.

These four nucleotides provide resonant frequencies for alpha, theta, and delta (the characteristic brain states going from consciousness to deep sleep).
This resonance relationship can be seen to link with helium inside the body
at various chemical sites.

The bridge connecting the solar system resonances and the brain frequencies
seem to reside in the DNA-RNA helix.

Oliver Reiser (University of Pittsburgh) developed a relationship between the
four helium cores in an atomic nucleus and the matrix forms on the DNA and
RNA. Reiser describes them as *"radiation belts of thought,"* the four "nucleotides" enter into the dynamics of these nuclear properties.

A *spheron* is a nuclear constituent roughly spherical in shape, and spaced in
concentric layers. The platonic solids are the five regular solids described by
Pythagoras now seen to form all crystal formations. These forms later became
the basis of the mathematics known as group theory. The so-called "resonances" were specific combinations of five regular solids geometry.

"*Helions*" is Pauling's term for spherons when he modeled the helium in the sun, the heliosphere around the Earth, and the hydrogen-helium plasma of the galactic disc. An optically activated molecule, such as helium, contains an electron which is coerced into a helical path by electric field.

This one-sided spiral is maintained in the intermolecular transport through protein molecules. Note that the protein units of "spherical viruses" are packed symmetrically in accordance with the pattern of cubic symmetry. Once more, we find our way back to Pythagoras and the Platonic solids!

8

ENLIGHTENMENT

SUN TRIGRAM

HISTORICAL CONTEXT — *The development of an ontology of mystical states allowed a roadmap toward higher consciousness. This meant a* **super soldier** *could become superior when union was made with his higher Self. With this layer of awareness, we could now move through life without constraint.*

It also resolved a question on the nature of free will and true will. Once that distinction was made, it set the limits of what was possible without reengineering the psychical body itself. With this nature of enlightenment, it allowed a physical universe where there were no mistakes (as in a **perfect soldier***).*

The historic context sets the stage for creating "enlightened" humans, superior on all levels of awareness. Like an Avatar, these protocols would allow us to take personal responsibility for one's own evolution.

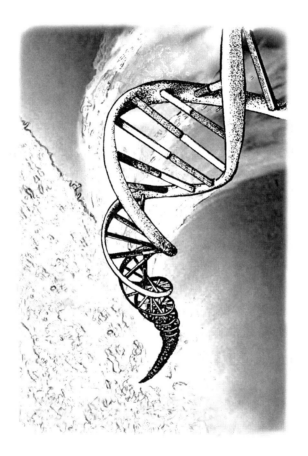

AS ABOVE SO BELOW

Chapter Eight

Mystical States of
Consciousness & Free Will

Robert Anton Wilson puts it best with his "right to guns and drugs" in California.
"Every man and woman wants to be a Tsar."

ROBERT ANTON WILSON'S *THE ILLUMINATI SERIES*

When I taught Parapsychology and Shamanism at the University of Washington in 1976, the only real books on the subject were mostly rehash of such works as Carlos Castaneda and various Brazilian Bruhos (sorcerers). I wanted something with more depth. That's when I discovered Dr. John Curtis Gowan's work at Northridge.

Gowan was a veteran educational psychologist whose primary work involved the fields of guidance, measurements, and gifted children. This led him toward the nature of creativity, and the first title in his all-important trilogy: "*The Development of the Creative Individual.*" This joining of the Erikson affected stages and the Piagetian cognitive stages unified Periodic Development Stage Theory, where creativity was identified as the cognitive development stage beyond formal operations.

The second book, "*The Development of the Psychedelic Individual,*" identified psychedelia (mind expansion) as the subsequent cognitive stage beyond creativity (corresponding with Eriksonian generativity period). This led him to write his third and most important book in the trilogy "Trance, Art, & Creativity."

Mystical States of Consciousness

This monumental trilogy led him to receive an international prize in psychology. The third book became a classic work on the ontology of mystical states and, eventually, to the development of the Northridge Development Test. This third book named three modes of contact between the conscious ego and the collective preconscious.

I used this third book for more than eight years, finding it absolutely consistent with my understandings of various mystical states and observed paranormal phenomena. It was basically a psychological analysis of the relationship between the Individual Ego and the Numinous Element in three basic modes: Prototaxic, Parataxic, and Syntaxic (modes of consciousness).

The taxonomy goes from a state of complete cognitive chaos (such as schizophrenia) through other types of dissociation and trance (which are regarded as prototaxic model). This, then, goes to a middle ground of parataxic modes which involves some amelioration of the relationship with the conscious ego through successive states of archetype, dream, ritual, and myth.

The final stage of consciousness, known as Art (Syntaxic mode), implies some cognitive control involving creativity, biofeedback, and meditation among others. Definitions are now needed to proceed with this ontology.

The Numinous Element - To begin this journey, one must postulate the existence of the numinous element, what Jung called the "*collective unconscious*" (also known as "*The Spirit of Man*"). The Aztecs called it "*Smoking Mirror*," which indicates an impersonal aspect. Also known as "*the clear light of the Void*," it tends to not be personal in nature.

For reference, one would never think of playing with high voltage electricity without the most careful insulation preparations. Similar precautions are also necessary with the numinous element. In the prototaxic mode, the require-ment is the excursion of ego-consciousness and the loss of memory of the en-counter. In parataxic mode, the matter is handled through ritual and images.

The Three Illusions - First discussed in Laurence LaShan monumental work *"The Medium, The Mystic, and the Physicist,"* the physical universe is associated with our ordinary states of consciousness and does not represent ultimate reality. Ultimate reality is also outside time as it is outside space.

Ultimate reality also transcends our sense of separate personal conscious-ness. Space, time and personal consciousness are thus the three illusions. It was Mark Twain who once said that every idea goes through three stages: "First people say it is impossible, and then they say it conflicts with the Bible, and finally they end up believing it."

Prototaxic Experience - Characterized by loss of ego known as Trance states of consciousness.

Parataxic Experience - Characterized by the production of images, whose meaning is not clear or categorical, known as Art (as a state of consciousness).

Syntaxic Experiences - Where meaning is more or less fully cognized symbol-ically, with ego present. This state is known as the Creative State of consciousness.

Ontology of Mystical States

Ontology is the study of what exists beyond the physical world and the nature of what exists. This is the realm of metaphysics (where *meta = beyond*). An epistemology, on the other hand, is the study of knowledge and justification. It offers a "reason" for your actions and is based strictly on values and your belief systems.

To determine which Laws of Nature exist, and what they are in and of them-selves is the domain of ontology. Trying to determine how we are justified in believing in these Laws of Nature, or believing anything about these Laws of Nature, is Epistemology.

'*What ought to be*' is derivable from '*What is*' through proper conduct of human reason. Or more precisely, it is about the proper conduct of interdisciplinary scholarships. This is taking personal responsibility for your own evolution. Its value is found in trying to understand your purpose of why things are the way they are, and then change them toward your Path.

Spirituality is not so much about what you do, but more about how you do it. It is the "character" part of Soul. It is the "*how you choose to do something.*" In metaphor, Ontology is a spiritual idea (such as eternity or consciousness), but without cause or a clear linear and logical definition. An epistemology has more to do with what is demonstrable.

With that, John Curtis Gowan developed his Ontology of Mystical States, offering a hierarchy for states of consciousness associated with paranormal (epistemology) confirmation. Just as ESP can be used for "critical decision-making power tools," this Ontology allows access to where consciousness *wants to evolve*. It is a *road-map* for *evolutionary states* of consciousness.

Ontology of Mystical States

John Curtis Gowan, *Table of Contents: Trance, Art, & Creativity,* c1975

Trance States of Consciousness

Schizophrenia
    Panic-Reaction
    Developmental Forcing
    Unstressing
Trance
    Group Trance Dance
    Possession Trance
    Mediumistic Trance
    Shamanistic Trance
        Initiation
        Paraphernalia and Familiars
        Magic
    Hypnosis
        Hysteria
        Autohypnosis and Autogenic Training
    Psychedelic Drugs
        Mescaline
        LSD
        Marijuana
        Delirium
    Sensory Deprivation
    ESP Effects
    Hallucinations
        Auditory
        Visual
        Hypnagognic
        Sensory Deprivation
        Death of Agent

Healing and the Conquest of Pain
      Folk Healing with Drugs (South America)
      Psychic Surgery
      Hypnotic Control of Pain
      Accelerated mental Process
Mastery of Fire
Psychokinesis and Poltergeist Phenomena
Out of Body Experience
Mob Contagion
Glossolalia
Xenoglossia
Single Limb Trance – Automatic Writing
Religious Trances

Art States of Consciousness

Archetypes
Dreams
    Nightmares
    Hypnotic Investigation of Dreams
    Dreams and Creativity
    Dreams and the Paranormal
    Lucid Dreams, High Dreams, and Programmed Dreams
Myth
    Myth and Animals
    Totemization of Myth
    Talismans
    Myth and Ritual
Ritual
Art
    Image Magic
    Art as Representation of the Numinous

Metaphysical Art
Art and Creativity

Creative States of Consciousness

The Three Illusions
The Right Cerebral Hemisphere Function
Siddhis
 ESP, Telepathy, Precognition, Psychometry,
  Accelerated Mental Process
 Human Auras and Kirlian Photography
 Healing and Anesthesia from Pain
 Power of Fire Psychic Heat
 OBE, Traveling Clairvoyance, Levitation, Magical Flight
 Psychokinesis
 Breathing, Autonomic Processes, Kundalini, Psychic Sound
Trantric Sex (Jhana-6)
Creativity (Jhana-5)
 Symbolization in Verbal Creativity
 Cognitive, Rational, and Semantic
 Personal and Environmental
 Psychological Openness
  Hypnosis
  Drugs
  ESP
  Dreams and Creativity
  Preconscious
  Self-Actualization
  Joy, Content, and Expectation of Good
  Serendipity
  Control of Environment
  Sense of Destiny

Yoga Forms

The word yoga is derived from the Sanskrit root yog which means "union" of "contact." Yoga is the science of the union of the human being with the divine that dwells within. The various great mystical texts of India, such as the Bhagavad-Gita, mention the following great divisions of Yoga.

Hatha Yoga – Ha means the moon and tha the sun. This branch of Yoga is concerned with the regularization or control of the breath. This is to modify the circulation of the prana or vital fluid in the physical body. By modifying prana, the yogi acts upon his psychic being, then on his mind, this is then modified. Thus, this is the yoga of physical exercises, or postures (asanas). This is essentially a Shivaist yoga.

Raja Yoga – Also known as royal yoga, it begins where Hatha yoga ends. Its emphasis is the mind, the goal being to direct the current of prana. Mental concentration plays an essential part. It is similar to Vishnu-forms of yoga.

Bhakti Yoga – This is the yoga of devotion, of love for the divine and for the guru who is its human form. Because of its devotional nature, this yoga is one of the most accessible to the Western mind.

Karma Yoga – This is also known as the yoga of action and is subdivided into a number of other yoga. This is the yoga of duty accomplished without affection, selfishness, or self-interest. It is exemplified in the great instruction given to Arjuna by Krishna in the Gita when the young prince, on the battlefield of Kurukshitra, hesitates before fighting.

Jnana Yoga – Also known as the yoga of knowledge, it is the intellectual realization of the divine that leads to an intuitive realization.

Any of the various yogas are superimposed one upon another. It is important for the student to have a teacher (or guru) for in following the practices at random and without direction, the student is liable to fall into a kind of psychic passivity, absolutely the opposite of the mystic experiences of yoga. The purpose of the teacher is to regulate the exercises and assign the method suitable to the individual disciple.

Tantric Yoga

Tantra is a spiritual method (or yoga) that takes into account both inner and outer realities. Derived from the root words meaning "to expand," "weave," or "extend consciousness," Tantra implies a form of continuity beyond the physical plane. Tantra teachings evolved in India and eventually spread to Nepal, Tibet, China, Japan, Thailand, and Indonesia.

These teachings are particularly relevant in this period of materialism and narcissism since all human activities can be used as tools in the Tantric path toward liberation. Tantra practices are a meditation system that aims at the experiences of the highest bliss in physical and spiritual relations by cultivating the totality of one's erotic potential.

Ancient scriptures containing the mystical teachings and ritual instructions of Tantra are called *tantras*. Briefly, they teach that earthly delights stem from the union of opposites and are achieved with an ideal partner. Such a union is said to exemplify the harmony of creation and be a step toward perfection (i.e., union with God). The power of love thus becomes central to the whole of existence.

Kama, or desire, is a creative principle that aims at the perfection of life on earth, just as the divine love that Krishna bore the shepherd girl Radha, represents the cosmic energies of creation in action on earth. Among the Tantric aids to meditation are mantras,. These are sacred sounds that may be visualized as yantras, and mandalas, symbols of psychic wholeness.

Kundalini is a Sanskrit word for the normally latent psychosexual power that, when awakened, ascends through the central channel of the subtle body. The root word kunda means "a pool or reservoir of energy." Kundalini is likened to a coiled snake, ready to strike at any moment.

When this energy is correctly directed, it can bring about cosmic consciousness and liberation. Various meditations for the awakening of Kundalini have been given for each herb in the Ritual Use section of my book, *The Magical and Ritual Use of Aphrodisiacs.*

The first action required by Tantric yoga is the cleansing of the nadis, the more highly developed nerve ganglia points in the body. These points have also been associated with the chakras but are really like tubes connecting the various chakra points. This purification is carried out by means of special body postures (asanas) and by breathing exercises (pranayama).

The mind is trained to concentrate itself upon a point or an object, real or imaginary, in order to remain calm and take the form that the will of the yogi wishes to impose upon it. This mental process is called Dhahran (concentration). When the mind can identify with the divine presence in every human being, a state called *Samadhi* has been reached.

Sex Magick

The alchemy described in the Tantric texts is often obscure and the secret door will not open to the uninitiated without a key. Rather than transmuting baser metals into gold, this alchemy actually takes place within the body. It is a hermetic distillation of actual bodily fluids, where the body itself provides all the instruments and utensils used by the alchemist.

By appropriating ritual movements, the gross substance within oneself can be transformed into the subtle quintessence that can reinvigorate the physical frame. Through a series of rituals, the body begins to "glow"; this activates supernatural faculties and puts the practitioner in communication with any entity in the universe. This naturally presupposes a complex system of subtle anatomy and physiology based on the charka or plexuses of the etheric body,

All power is promised to those who can siphon the lower energy toward the upper, but this is almost impossible for the layman. A tremendous need for discipline is required, discipline that is usually beyond the capacity of the average individual. A sympathetic resonance does exist between the chakras, however. By Tantric methods, the Kundalini can be made to blaze up through the chakras, igniting each until this stream of flame reaches the crown (or *sahasrara* chakra).

One rite commonly celebrated in many Tantric sects is known as the chakra-puja, or circle worship. The participants sit in a circle, alternating male and female, implying complete mutual equality among those present. One couple sits in the center of the circle. A ceremonial meal consisting of wine, meat, fish, and bread is followed by a rite of sexual intercourse. Those food items represent certain fundamental categories equated with the elements and the interior faculties of the body.

Wine symbolizes fire and the subtle draught of immortality that the Tantric must learn to distill and drink. Meat symbolizes air and the bodily functions that must be brought under control. Fish represents water and the techniques of sexual occultism. Breath is the earth, or the natural environment, which must be understood and controlled.

Sexual intercourse (*maithuna*) symbolizes ether, the quintessence of all the elements, and is a means to the final goal of all Tantric endeavors. Through it one apprehends the ultimate reality. The sex act in its normal, gross form may occasionally bring a fleeting revelation eternal truth, but that would be rare, as the smoke of passion usually clouds the mind.

Sex, as a sacred ritual unclouded by passion, can reveal being, expand consciousness, and confer true bliss. The way through pleasure (*bhukti*) can lead one to redemption (*mukti*). Sex, from this perspective, can be a way of salvation. This is the basis of the secret of tantra.

On the Practice of Ritual and Ceremony

There are three phases of every ritual process:
1. Separation from profane or daily life
2. The transition stage, or twilight zone, which lies between
3. The new order or perception of reality that occurs in the
   sacred time of the soul.

The in-between, or twilight zone, creates a state of receptivity. Ritual acts re-awaken deep layers of the psyche and bring the mythological or archetypal ideas back to memory. Magic is the transition from passivity to activity in which the will is essential. By contrast, schizophrenic magic is not followed by realistic action; the fantasy is a substitute for action where the ego should be weak or even absent.

Ritual is often considered the celebration of a myth. Myth functions as a paradigm or model. In this school of thought, the construct of a ritual can be seen as the enactment of the myth, the myth being recognized as the source of all action. Myth is a dynamic expression of the motivational power of the archetype at its core.

The main value of ritual is for the soul. Ritual can be defined as an imitation of a numinous element (or god form) in the life of the aspirant. Ritual can be seen as the outward or visible form of contact or as an epiphany with an inward or spiritual grace. It is essentially a metaphorical expression of creative imagination.

The symbol always starts on the inside as a form of consciousness and is projected outward. Magical rituals contain basic elements that appear in approximately the following sequence:

1. Setting up the circle to define a working area.
2. A form of banishing to clear the working area and help concentration and focusing.
3. Middle Pillar exercise to bring in light and build up libido or magical potency. This helps participants visualize their subtle body or body of light.

4. Invocation is the "calling in" of the desired god form or attributes in an attempt at self-transformation.

5. Changing of a Eucharist with the energy of the god form and its consumption as an epiphany with the god.

6. Meditative period.

7. Banishing to return the aspirant to normal consciousness.

8. Closing the temple.

These steps may be expanded to include divination, dance, dramatic scenarios, or sex magic acts. Any appropriate gestures may be added (like massage or mudras), but none of these basics can be omitted without incurring the peril of exposing the soul to random forces.

The purpose of ritual lies in its expression as an art form. Partaking in its performance is an end in itself. The spiritual import lies in the quality with which the ritual is conducted. Ritual, as symbolic action, is the enactment of mythic patterns for the sheer joy of the relationship with the archetypal dimension.

Remember, the purpose of the ritual is an end in itself. This can leave no room for rationalizing the need for results.

The Magick of the Temple of the Orient

The first use of sex within the rituals of western traditions of magic began with the *Ordo Templi Orientis* (O.T.O.), an 800-year-old Masonic order in Germany. Members had studied the Hindu traditions of Tantra and found the energy contained in those rituals was greater than in any other known technique.

At the turn of the century, Aleister Crowley became their new Outer Head of the Order (O.H.O.) and rewrote those rituals for a more contemporary application. For a clear picture of this technique, it is recommended that the student first read chapter 16 of *The Tree of Life* by Israel Regardie, followed by pages 82-86 of Liber Aleph, *The Book of Wisdom or Folly* by Aleister Crowley.

The *"Mass of the Holy Ghost"* is described on page 86:

de Formula Tota
On the complete formula.

Here then is thy Schedule for all Operations of Magick.

> *First: thou shalt discover thy True Will, as I have already taught thee, and that Bud therefore which is the Purpose of this Operation*

> *Next, formulate this Bud-Will as a Person, seeking or constructing it, and naming it, according to thine Holy Qabalah, and its infallible Rule of Truth.*

> *Third: Purify and consecrate this Person, concentrating upon him, and against all else. This Preparation shall continue in all thy daily Life. Mark well: make ready a New Child immediately after every Birth.*

> *Fourth: make an especial and direct Invocation at thy Mass, before the Introit, formulating a visible Image of this Child, and offering the Right of Incarnation.*

> *Fifth: perform the Mass, not omitting the Ipiklesis and let there be a Golden Wedding Ring at the Marriage of thy Lion and thine Eagle.*

> *Sixth: at the Consumption of the Eucharist accept this Child, loosing thy Consciousness in him, until he be well assimilated within thee.*

Now then do this continuously, for by Repetition cometh fourth both Strength and Skill, and the Effect is cumulative, if thou allow no time for it to dissipate itself.

We will now describe in simple terms how this formula is applied to sex magic:

1. Discover your true will. What is the purpose of the operation? Or, perhaps you wish to have some event occur, etc.

2. "Name it" – as a person, an entity which has its own personality. It could be that wish to change a habit. If that is the case, then treat this new proposed change as a new entity, a new person who is not you. This is the detail to the purpose.

3. Purify and consecrate this new person. This is the point where you and your mate generate the desire, the foreplay, with each reminding the other continuously of the purpose of the operation. This is the bud-will.

4. Formulate an image of this bud-will into a child (magical child). With entry, you both begin to redefine the child. The proper term for this is synergy: the creation of new information to add and supplement the original intent. It is the invocation. You begin to live what you create. For visualization, the Red Lion is the male essence and the White Eagle is the female men strum.

5. Form a bond with the gold ring. This is the climax! The Red Lion becomes the White Lion and the White Eagle becomes the Red Eagle.

6. Consume the Eucharist and know that no other energy is necessary. After the climax, both male and female should eat the semen and menstrum. The Eucharist "in alchemical terms" is the Philosopher's Stone.

Note: *The thought during a sexual climax .... happens!*
(This is the Masonic secret)

Purpose of Magick

People who take a major mind alternant are actually performing an act of magic. The first and most important question that should be asked is, "Why am I performing this act?" In other words, "What is the goal?" Classical Hinduism suggests four possibilities:

1. Increased personal power, intellectual understanding, improvement in life situation or insight into "self."
2. Duty, to help others, providing care or rehabilitation. Healing.
3. Fun, sensuous enjoyment and pure experience.
4. Transcendence, liberation from the three basic illusions: space, time, and ego. Attainment of mystical union.

Once a goal has been selected and defined, the next most important question should then be asked: "What is your method of reprogramming?" I recommend reading "*The Psychedelic Experience*" by Timothy Leary. This manual guides one through the intermediate states between death and rebirth.
It systematically lists the levels of consciousness met after normal consciousness leaves the place of routine reality. It attempts to forewarn and prepare the voyager for the range of visions to be encountered. Leary's manual is based on the *Bardo Thodol*.

The *Bardo Thodol*, which first appeared in English as the *Tibetan Book of the Dead* in 1927, is used in Tibet as a breviary to be read or recited on the occasion of death to help the dying person concentrate on the experience he or she is about to undergo. It is a road map to the cycles of events after death that leads to either liberation or reincarnation.

In highly symbolic language, the spirit is told what to expect in each of the three stages between death and rebirth. The first stage describes psychic happenings at the moment of death; the second stage describes the dream state that follows and the "karmic" illusions that occur; and the third step describes the beginning of prenatal feelings, or the return of the ego.

Leary's *The Psychedelic Experience* is the perfect book written for this form of magic. He has modularized each point correctly, including the ability to literally create rebirth! With this manual, one can actually reprogram attitudes, behavior patterns, and goals in life.

Autarchy

The term autarchy is synonymous with autocracy, the system of government where power is held by an individual. An autocracy is a form of government in which the political power is held by a single person. The term is derived from the Greek word autokratôr (lit. *"self-ruler"*, *"ruler of one's self"*).

Autocracy is not synonymous with totalitarianism, as this concept was precisely forged to distinguish modern regimes that appeared in the 1930s from traditional dictatorships. It also isn't synonymous with military dictatorship, as these often take the form of *"collective presidencies."*

However, an autocracy may be totalitarian or be a military dictatorship. But, it may also be a liberal autocracy governed by an *"enlightened despot"* who allows a significant amount of individual rights, such as freedom of speech and private property.

The term monarchy differs in that it emphasizes the hereditary characteristic, though some Slavic monarchs traditionally included the title *"autocrat"* as part of their official styles. The actual power of the monarch may be limited.

Historically, many monarchs ruled autocratically but, eventually, their power was diminished and dissolved with the introduction of constitutions giving the people the power to make decisions for themselves through elected bodies of government.

The autocrat needs some kind of power structure to rule. Only a boss of a street gang or a barbarian chieftain can truly rule with only his personal charisma and his fighting skills. Most historical autocrats depended on their nobles, the military, the priesthood or others, who could turn against the ruler and depose or murder him. The true nature of a historical autocracy can be difficult to judge.

Free Will

Philosophers have debated this question for over two thousand years and just about everyone has had something to say about it. Most philosophers now basically agree that the concept of free will is very closely connected to the concept of moral responsibility. Acting with free will, on such views, is just to satisfy the metaphysical requirement on being responsible for one's action.

But the significance of free will is always about its connection to moral responsibility. Free will also appears to be a condition on one's accomplishments. This is why sustained effort and creative work are praise-worthy. It is also about the value we accord to love and friendship

Philosophers who distinguish *freedom of action and freedom of will* do so because success in carrying out goals often depends on factors wholly beyond our control. There are always external constraints on the range of options we can meaningfully try to undertake. As the presence or absence of these conditions (and constraints) is not our responsibility, it is plausible that the central loci of our responsibilities are about choices.

If there is such a thing as free will it has many dimensions (like consciousness). Free will is also about the deliberate choosing on the basis of desires and values. Philosophers (since Plato) have commonly distinguished the 'animal' and 'rational' parts of our nature, with the latter implying a great deal more psychological complexity.

Our rational nature includes our ability to judge some ends as 'good' (or worth pursuing) and value them even though satisfying them may lead to unpleasantness. Such judgments need not be based on moral values. More plausible is the suggestion that one acts with free will when one's deliberation is *sensitive* to one's own judgments concerning what is best in the circumstances, whether or not one acts upon such a judgment.

There are two general theories on free will that are based on the capacity to deliberate about possible actions in the light of one's conception of the good.

First, there are agents who deliberately choose to act as they do, but who are motivated to do so by a compulsive, controlling sort of desire. Such agents are not willing freely.

Secondly, a person's psychology can be externally manipulated by another agent (example: neuro-physiological implant) causing to desire strongly a particular action which previously was not disposed to be chosen. The deliberative process could be perfectly normal, reflective, and rational, but seemingly not freely made.

A more moderate grouping within the self-determination approach to free will allows that beliefs, desires, and external factors all can causally influence the act of free choice itself.

Determinism

The controversy over the concept of free will is the question of whether or not actions are consciously controlled or merely witnessed. This problem requires understanding the relation between freedom and causation and determining whether or not the laws of nature are causally deterministic. So, for instance, hard determinists argue that the universe is deterministic and that this makes free will impossible.

The principle of free will has religious, ethical, and scientific implications. For example, in the religious realm, free will may imply that an omnipotent divinity does not assert its power over individual will and choices.

In ethics, it may imply that individuals can be held morally accountable for their actions. In the scientific realm, it may imply that the actions of the body, including the brain and the mind, are not wholly determined by physical causality. Determinism is roughly defined as the view that all current and future events are necessitated by past events combined with the laws of nature.

CNV

The *contingent negative variation* (CNV) was one of the first event-related potential (ERP) components to be described. The CNV component was first described by Dr. W. Grey Walter in 1964. The CNV effect (*or readiness potential*) is a negative spike of electrical activity that appears in the brain half a second prior to a person being consciously aware of movements that he is about to make.

The importance of this finding was that it was one of the first studies which showed this activity could be related to a cognitive process such as expectancy. It is an increasing negative shift of the cortical electrical potentials associated with an anticipated response to an expected stimulus. It is an electrical event indicative of a state of readiness or expectancy.

Walter and colleagues also noticed that electric responses to warning stimuli seemed to have three phases: a brief positive component, a brief negative component, and a sustained negative component. They noticed that the brief components varied due to sensory modality, while the sustained component varied with the contingency between the warning and imperative stimuli and the attention of the subject.

They labeled this component the *"contingent negative variation"* because the variation of the negative wave was contingent on the statistical relationship between the warning and imperative stimuli.

In a series of experiments in the 1980s, Benjamin Libet studied the relationship between conscious experience of volition and the CNV, and found that the BP started about 0.35 seconds earlier than the subject's reported conscious awareness that 'now he or she feels the desire to make a movement.'

He concluded that we have no free will in the initiation of our movements; though, since subjects were able to prevent intended movement at the last moment, we do have a veto. Intriguingly, this effect brings into question the very notion of consciousness or free will, and should be considered as part of a person's overall reaction time to events.

True Will

This is a term found within the mystical system of *Thelema* - established in 1904 with Aleister Crowley's writing of *The Book of the Law*. He defines it as a person's grand destiny (purpose) in life. It is also the moment to moment path of action that operates in perfect harmony with nature (flow).

This *Will* does not spring from conscious intent, but from the interplay between the deepest Self and the entire Universe. Therefore, the enlightened *Thelemite* is one who is able to eliminate, or bypass, ego-created desires, conflicts, and habits, and tap directly into the Self/Universe nexus. At this point, the *Thelemite* acts in alignment with nature, just as a stream flows downhill, with neither resistance nor *"lust of result."*

Thelema

Thelema roughly means *"will"* in Greek. It is also one of four words in Greek for the different forms of love. They are *Eros* (physical), *Philo* (emotional), *Agape* (Intellectual), and *Thelema* (archetypal). The highest form (*Thelema*) is actually the *love of will*, to represent your *purpose* with conscious awareness (Path of Life).

The phrase *True Will* does not appear in the *Book of the Law,* the central sacred text of *Thelema*. Nevertheless, Aleister Crowley's various commentaries on the Book routinely postulate that each individual has a unique and incommensurable *True Will* that determines his or her proper course in life.

This invention of Crowley's appears to be an attempt to explain how some actions may be wrong (or "false") when *"There is no law beyond Do what thou wilt."* Actions that conform to *True Will* are considered to be correct, while *willed actions* that deviate from *True Will* may, nevertheless, be considered wrong.

By definition, an aspirant's True Will must fit the aspirant's nature. Crowley defines True Will as the will which does not *"rest content with things partial and transitory, but ... proceed[s] firmly to the End."* He also defines *"the End, ...as the destruction of oneself in Love."* This place is known as *"being enflamed."*

Quotations from Aleister Crowley

"The most common cause of failure in life is ignorance of one's own True Will, or of the means by which to fulfill that Will."
(from Magick, Book 4, p. 127)

"A man who is doing his True Will has the inertia of the Universe to assist him."
(from Magick, Book 4, p.128)

"One cannot do one's True Will intelligently unless one knows what it is."
(from Magick, Book 4, p.174)

"Know firmly, O my Son, that the True Will cannot err; for it is thine appointed Course in Heaven, in whose Order is Perfection."
(from Liber Aleph, p. 13)

"True Will should spring, a fountain of Light, from within, and flow unchecked, seething with Love, into the Ocean of Life."
(from Little Essays Towards Truth, p.76)

The Ethical Man Versus The Moral Man

"The ethical man knows what is right; the moral man does what is right."
- ANONYMOUS

On the TV show NCIS the character of Dr. "Ducky" Mallard gives a good example of this idea: *"The ethical man knows he shouldn't cheat on his wife, whereas the moral man actually wouldn't."*

The next question is are you ethical or moral? In the Book of James in the Bible it states, "*Therefore, to him who knows to do good and does not do it, to him it is sin.*" – James 4:17 (NKJV). If we know what is right, yet do not do what is right, we are living in sin.

Let us be true believers, living lives of true morality.

On the True Nature of Things

Because man does not have "*total awareness,*" he cannot (by definition) have *free will*. He also does not have rights (to *free will*); what he does have are "*responsibilities.*" If he wants to enjoy freedom, he has a responsibility to be free. *Free will* (like freedom) can only come from his evolution of consciousness.

Our purpose is to discover our individual (and unique) *true will*, and then take the *responsibility*, to evolve that awareness to the next level. The tools described in this book were developed to make supermen (for the military), and they work. Now, you have a "first-system" of tools for use. Your purpose is to begin that journey toward the evolution of your own consciousness.

Freedom without accountability or responsibility can only lead to tyranny. You must develop a *moral responsibility* for this personal evolution – because men are built, not born.

That is the *true nature* of the *will* in man.

Index

absorption, 23, 28

alpha, 42, 43, 44, 46, 47, 49, 50, 53, 67, 143, 187, 189, 192, 195, 211, 222

altered states, 43, 51, 64, 118, 149, 181, 200

amplitude, 45, 49, 67, 193

amygdala, 200, 201, 204

antibiotics, 16, 21, 28, 31, 32, 37, 38

archetype(s), 61, 62, 64, 66, 68, 96, 99, 151, 154, 155, 156, 157, 158, 159, 160, 161, 162, 163, 164, 165, 166, 167, 168, 169, 176, 177, 178, 206, 208, 210, 211, 216, 220, 227

ATP, 17, 26

audio, 39, 43, 55, 68, 75, 85, 86, 87, 89, 170, 188, 190, 191, 192, 193, 194, 196, 197, 198

bacteria, 21, 30, 31, 37, 38, 83

balance, 22, 31, 62, 75, 76, 92, 111, 163, 184

belief(s), 6, 11, 93, 99, 101, 102, 103, 104, 105, 106, 107, 108, 109, 110, 112, 114, 115, 120, 145, 147, 162, 184, 217, 234

beta, 45, 49, 187, 192

beta-glucans, 16, 17

binaural beat, 188, 189, 190, 192, 193, 194, 195

biofeedback, 3, 39, 41, 43, 44, 50, 51, 52, 54, 68, 71, 144, 181, 197, 216, 222

biofeedback research, 44, 51, 52, 68

biofeedback techniques, 44, 52

blood, 19, 23, 24, 26, 27, 32, 34, 35, 41, 42, 44, 48, 51, 52, 53, 80, 81, 82, 83, 172

brain, 8, 9, 10, 39, 41, 42, 43, 44, 45, 46, 48, 49, 51, 52, 54, 55, 56, 57, 59, 60, 61, 62, 63, 65, 66, 68, 69, 82, 83, 85, 86, 87, 88, 91, 92, 95, 107, 110, 116, 120, 127, 136, 138, 144, 145, 146, 181, 183, 184, 186, 187, 188, 189, 190, 191, 192, 193, 194, 195, 196, 197, 198, 199, 200, 201, 202, 203, 204, 205, 206, 207, 209, 210, 211, 234, 235

brain activity, 10, 42, 199, 202, 203

brain drivers, 196, 197, 198

brain frequencies, 48, 60, 206, 211

brain metabolism, 42, 43

brain wave patterns, 44, 45, 46, 52

brain waves, 44, 45, 52, 54

breath control, 73, 75, 82, 85

breathing, 25, 76, 77, 79, 80, 81, 82, 83, 84, 97, 107, 183, 209, 221, 225

cancer, 13, 16, 17, 19, 24, 25, 30, 33, 37, 38, 121, 122

239

Other Publications by
Dr. Richard Alan Miller

Workbook 1
Exercise Supplement for Power Tools for the 21st Century

$12.00
6x9"; delux color soft cover; black and white interior; 68 pages; contains explanitory
illustrations and historic photos from the author's past during the time of his Navy SEAL
curriculum development.
ISBN 978-0-9883379-2-3
Author: Dr. Richard Alan Miller

An exercise supplement for the 2nd book in the series Toward the Evolution of Consciousness this book features eight main training focuses. It includes self testing exercises,
systems of cosmology and philosophy at the heart of developing one's consciousness and
clearly defined meditation practices to achieve your goals.

These are the protocols that were developed for the Navy SEALs to create super soldiers.
these Power Tools can be used today for your own personal evolution of consciousness.

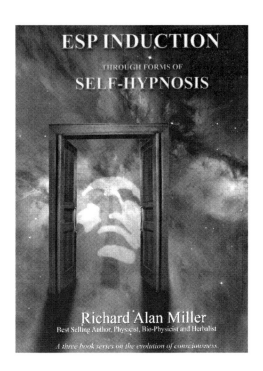

ESP Induction
Through Forms of Self-Hypnosis

$18.00
6x9"; delux color soft cover; black and white interior; 214 pages; illustrated.
ISBN 978-1-890693-30-5
Author: Dr. Richard Alan Miller

The first book in the three book series written by Dr. Richard Alan Miller — Toward the Evolution of Consciousness, and an how-to book intended to increase a person's intuition and extra sensory perception (ESP) or sixth sense. The protocols identified here have been tested and found reliable in increasing a person's intuition or guessing ability by up to 400% above an individual's beginning levels. The book introduces basic information on self-hypnosis as a tool fir enhancing our latent human potentils or, as they are referred to in some military literature these days our anomalous human potentials peviously called ESP.

These are the protocols that were developed for the Navy SEALs to create super soldiers. these Power Tools can be used today for your own personal evolution of consciousness.

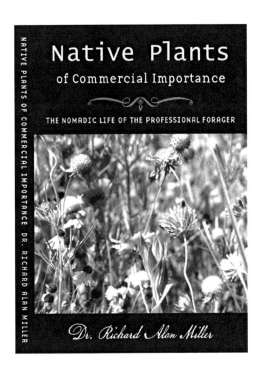

Native Plants of Commercial Importance
The Nomadic Life of the Professional Forager
A book for the Wildcrafter and Herb Farmer

$20.00
6x9"; delux color soft cover; black and white interior; 344 pages; fully illustrated.
ISBN 978-0-9883379-0-9
Author: Dr. Richard Alan Miller

Here is an information-filled look at how to supplement rural incomes by the harvest of native plants from the region. Among the wild plants of North America are many which have long been used in medicinal, cosmetic, food and floral industries. Some of them are used in sufficient quantities to make them commercially important.

The book describes these and other forest products, dividing North America into five regions: Northeast, South, Midwest, Southwest and the Northwest. Each region contains a descriptions of 10 common crops now harvested, with detail and a special appendix on marketing. Reforestation is stressed to make each crop renewable and self-generating as a natural resource. This technique has led to the new concept of Forest Farming.

The future of foraging as a source of supplementing one's rural income lies with our ability to recognize natural resources.

The Encyclopedia for Alternative Agriculture
For Urban and Semi-Rural Communities

$24.95
Large format, 8.5x11"; delux color soft cover; black and white interior; 216 pages.
ISBN 978-0-9883379-1-6
Author: Dr. Richard Alan Miller

The Encyclopedia of Alternative Agriculture: For the Urban and Semi-Rural Communities
is an anthology of approximately 120 newsletters over a 10 year period called, The Herb
Market Report. Each issue features 2 herbs, one on small farm alternatives and the other
on a forage crop. Each also includes a farm/forage plan, harvest and drying techniques,
processing and storage requirements, and marketing options. A cottage industry section
is featured as well. The articles are in depth, concerning all aspects of herb production,
processing and marketing for active and potential herb farmers.They teach the basics for
how to "small farm" field crops correctly, and be successful. Book 1 contains the first 24
newsletters.

*The author, Dr. Richard Alan Miller, is a world renowned agricultural consultant and re-
searcher on the forefront and 'cutting edge' of the sciences related to botanicals and their
practical cultivation, use and marketing.*

Dr. Richard Alan Miller is a pioneer in the annals of metaphysical and paranormal exploration. Miller began working in the "X-Files" world of Navy Intel (Seal Corp. and then MRU) in the late 60's. His public collaborations and research continue.

As an original black ops team-member, Miller's research in the field of paranormal began as a graduate physicist working 11 years with Navy Intel (Anesthesiology). During this period numerous foundational papers, including "*A Holographic Concept of Reality*" and "*Embryonic Holography*" were written.

His past and current writings and presentations reveal a depth of knowledge and practical experience in three major fields; Alternative Agriculture, New Age Physics, and Metaphysics.

Miller now writes for Nexus magazine and is a preferred guest on internet radio. He is re-emerging at a critical time in humanities evolution where metaphysics and practical survival converge.

For a full listing of publications for sale, the current schedule and blog reports please go to www.richardalanmiller.com.

CPSIA information can be obtained at www.ICGtesting.com
Printed in the USA
BVOW07s1711080114

341104BV00004B/23/P